THE STORY LIVES
LEADING A MISSIONAL REVOLUTION

Let your story live!

Henriët Schapelhouman

Henriët

Matt 25:21

Tendril Press
DENVER, COLORADO

Published by Tendril Press™
© 2013 All Rights Reserved
www.TendrilPress.com
PO Box 441110 Aurora, CO 80044
303.696.9227

ISBN 978-0-9858933-0-9 Paper

Library of Congress Control Number: 2012945445

Scripture quoted from BibleGateway.com

Scripture quotations marked CEV are taken from the Holy Bible, Contemporary English Version® Copyright © 1991, 1992, 1995 by American Bible Society. Used by permission. All rights reserved.

Scripture quotations marked ESV are taken from the Holy Bible, English Standard Version® (ESV®), Copyright © 2001 by Crossway, a publishing ministry of Good News Publishers. Used by permission. All rights reserved.

Scripture quotations marked MSG are taken from the The Message. Copyright © 1993, 1994, 1995, 1996, 2000, 2001, 2002. Used by permission of NavPress Publishing Group. All rights reserved.

Scripture quotations marked NIV are taken from the Holy Bible, NEW INTERNATIONAL VERSION®, NIV® Copyright © 1973, 1978, 1984, 2011 by Biblica, Inc.™ Used by permission. All rights reserved worldwide.

Scripture quotations marked NLT are taken from the Holy Bible, New Living Translation, Copyright © 1996, 2004, 2007. Used by permission of Tyndale House Publishers, Inc., Carol Stream, Illinois 60188. All rights reserved.

Scripture quotations marked TLB are taken from the Holy Bible, The Living Bible, Copyright © 2012. Used by permission of Tyndale House Publishers, Inc., Carol Stream, Illinois 60188. All rights reserved.

Cover Photo: ©iStockphoto.com/coloroftime; Photographer, Cris
Author Photo: Brant Photographers, Inc., Bellevue, WA Photographer: Rob Rose

Individual Sales. This book is available through most bookstores, online bookstores, or can be ordered directly from the publisher. Special discounts are available for quantity purchases by churches, organizations, associations, and others. For details, contact the "Special Sales Department" at the publisher's address above.

Art Direction, Book Design © 2012.
All Rights Reserved by

 A J Images Inc.,
www.AJImagesInc.com
Info@AJImagesInc.com

To Jesus,
my Lord and my friend,
who gave me true life:

You've bought me with the ultimate prize.
I'm not my own. I pray that his book and my life
bring you honor and glory, and pleases you.

His master replied, 'Well done, good and faithful servant!
You have been faithful with a few things; I will put you in charge
of many things. Come and share your master's happiness!'

—Matthew 25:21, NIV

Contents

Foreword

I have a story to tell. Correct that. I am a story, whether I tell it or not. Those who study the connection between our identity and the stories we tell ourselves inform us that we are our stories—that the ability to tell ourselves a story of ourselves is how we make sense of the life we live. So, yes, I have and am a story. Who I am, created by God, is shaped by all my influences—from the times in southern Illinois when my parents named me and brought me home and nurtured me among two sisters…to my public schooling days, filled as they were with sports and friends…to my church, filled as it was with the comforts of knowing we were headed for eternal life when we died and fellowship with one another in the here and now…to college and seminary and doctoral studies… to marriage to Kris and nurturing two children, Laura and Lukas, now married with some grandchildren…to my days as a professor and a writer and a preacher and a baseball coach and a golfer and a neighbor. These make up my story and make me who I am. Without that story, I'd be someone else.

We all have a story to tell because each of us—including you—is the product of our influences, though yours are different than mine, even if they overlap in important ways. Sometimes it amazes me that we can communicate with one another. If you add up all the separable influences you have and we have, and how different they can be, there's a bit of a miracle that we can communicate meaningfully with one another. We were recently in Iceland, a country about as far north on the map as one can get, and we had no problem communicating. Their story connected quite comfortably with my story.

The reason I have a story and we all have a story is because God has made us part of the Story God is creating in this world. Deep inside we know there's something that connects us all, and that connection also connects us with God, and that Story is that God made us—however God made us is a debate we needn't worry about in this context—and made us for himself and for ourselves and for one another in such a way that connection to God and to one another makes each of our stories come alive in ways they would not otherwise have life.

At the heart of God's Story is Jesus Christ—his life, his death, his resurrection, his exaltation—and in that singular Story we find the clue to our Story. Henriët knows this, and that's why she has written this fine book about learning to tell our stories. Her approach, however, is not to say "whatever story you've got is the true story" but to say that our stories make most sense when they connect to God and to God's Story in Jesus Christ. Henriët, then, wants each of our stories to come alive so they can be our best story as a story that fits into God's great Story.

As you read *The Story Lives*, may I suggest that you not breeze through it looking for something special, or for a sermon illustration. Ponder the questions at the end of each chapter and let them take you where an expert in story-telling will take you: to God, to God's Story and therefore back to you and to us so that we, together, can come alive to declare the goodness of God's Story.

Scot McKnight
Professor of New Testament
Northern Seminary

Acknowledgements

The writing of *The Story Lives* has been its own ten-year journey. Many contributed to this work in various ways. I'm grateful to those who most influenced me to have a Kingdom mindset. These include my professors at Fuller Theological Seminary, as well as friends and authors.

The following people I consider most influential in changing my thinking: Scot McKnight—you inspired me to live the Jesus Creed. Reggie McNeal—it's really all your fault! You opened my eyes to missional leadership. Robert Freeman and Ron Hannaford—thank you for starting the Master of Arts in Global Leadership program. It changed my life! David Kopp—you taught me to write and inspired me to go back to school. Thank you!

Others who transformed my thinking and missional leading are George Barna and Kevin Mannoia (thanks for ordaining me!).

I am grateful to my friends who have believed in me:
- Cindy Patterson. I appreciate you as my fellow pastor and guinea pig, and for being my true and honest friend. Thank you!

- Nancy Nelson. I would not have attended the Christian Writer's Conference without you. Thank you for your prayers...they carried me through.

- Rita Nussli. Thank you for stretching me, investing in me, and teaching me to go deeper with Jesus. You are amazing.

- Tamara Buchan, fellow pastor and author. You told me to finish the book and put me in contact with Tendril Press, Karin Hoffman and Cecile Higgins. You helped make it happen!

❧ Tammie Fuchs, Cheryl Fontana, Els Mengler—my true, faithful and life-long friends. Thanks for always being there for me and cheering me on.

❧ Semper Vita Communities. You are a picture of true community in Jesus. Thank you for the honor of learning from you, growing with you and going missional together. Thank you for your prayers.

❧ Semper Vita Board and supporters. You believed in the vision of this book. Thank you for supporting me through the process.

I am deeply indebted and eternally grateful to my family who has put up with my passion and drive for God's Kingdom:

❧ To my dad, Luuk de Bly, the writer in the family, for passing on the gift and passion. I'm sorry you are not here to see this work completed.

❧ To my mom, Dina de Bly Dijkxhoorn, for always being there for me and shaping my love for God with your many readings of *The Children's Bible*. Everyone should hear her read.

❧ To my sister, Suzanne Lercel, the artist of our family, for cheering me on and allowing me to practice living my faith on her.

❧ To my husband, Fred, my biggest fan and faithful supporter. You are so kind and steady. I love you! You're always willing to help me so I can do ministry, writing, or any other endeavor. Thank you for reading and re-reading. This book would not have happened without you.

❧ To my son, Harrison, for being a miracle in my life and teaching me about God's love for his children and for people who do not yet belong to him. I love you so much.

Introduction

Long before God gave me the title, *The Story Lives*, the message of this book percolated in my heart and mind. Decades ago, God planted the seed, and then he wove a tapestry of experiences and information culminating into this work. As you read these chapters, I pray you'll experience the urgency to know and tell our stories so people may know Jesus.

God taught me about his heart for people far way from him through experiencing the heart crushing pain of watching loved ones turn their backs on God. One soul wrenching night when I cried to God in deep anguish about a beloved family member, God impressed on me that my feelings mirrored how he felt about each of his lost children.

Wow! In a strange way, it comforted me that painful night, but God's truth also broke my heart for what breaks his heart. God gave me a glimpse of his heart. He deposited a tiny bit of his passion and love for people far away from him and placed it on my heart. Many people live without knowing him or his love. After that night, I have never looked at people the same way again.

What Is a Missional Life?

God invites all of us, but especially Christian leaders, to live missionally. Living missionally lets us practically fulfill the Great Commission, tangibly be the hands and feet of Jesus, and demonstrate who Jesus is.

How Can We Live Missionally?

We live missionally by demonstrating our stories incarnationally and intentionally within our contexts.

When God opened my eyes to living missionally, the course of my life completely changed. I rediscovered in new and deeper ways, God's commandment to love him, love other Christians, and love my neighbors. He made me and sends me to live authentically. All I have to do is be myself and live my story missionally so God can use me to bring people to himself. This truth is amazing, and the truth applies to all of us!

Each of us has a story to tell. We're the only ones who can tell it! Our stories are bigger than each of us—much bigger. Each of our stories is part of the story, Jesus' story. He lives so his story lives. He lives through our stories and our lives. We can say as we live, "The Story" lives.

What Would a Missional Life Look Like?

Every one of our stories fits into God's great love story of creation, salvation, reconciliation, and restoration. God gave us our stories for his purposes, yet many of us live without ever accomplishing all that God designed for us. Why? Because most of our faith stories are lived in boxes, church boxes, hiding God's wonderful "Good News story" of Jesus' love and life from the world around us.

The question is: will you tell your story for you or for Jesus? What if we lived our stories beyond the "church" boxes and practically demonstrated God's love and Jesus' life to a hungry and thirsty world? Could our stories take on greater significance and purpose? Could our lives have the effect and meaning that we all so greatly desire?

Every Christian leader is sent to tell his or her unique story in community to advance Jesus' Kingdom. My goal is to help leaders live out their stories to create a missional army of empowered leaders to affect every community for Christ. I desire us to fuel the missional revolution to bring people into a relationship with Jesus.

Gain a New Perspective!

For over twenty years, I have been in full or part-time ministry. When I was pastor of adult ministries at a sizable, local church, I attempted to plug people into the community through volunteering. We desired to connect people to existing opportunities, as well as provide church sponsored opportunities. I realized my view was too small. My ultimate desire and motivation was to reach people with the love of Jesus so that they would find him and then come to our church. God broke me out of that mold and showed me that even though my heart was for the community, I was still peering through the windows of the box, our church. I remained focused on the box rather than on the Kingdom of God.

As Christian leaders, we tend to look through the church lens, and we often miss truly touching people in our neighborhoods and life contexts with the love of Jesus. People are hungry for God, and Christians desire to demonstrate God's love, but often we can't connect those two dots. How can we accomplish both?

One "place" where people in our neighborhoods gather today is through community involvement and volunteer opportunities. If we get involved and volunteer, we can easily connect with people in natural and organic ways. However, it will take leaders to propel this missional revolution from church huddles to community gatherings.

Who Should Read This Book?

The Story Lives is written for serious, missionally-minded leaders at all levels of ministry, both in local churches and beyond, who want to take the missional conversation from theory to action. Every chapter starts with a pertinent story. Each of the stories is based on real people in real situations experiencing life and experiencing Jesus. Missional leaders who are people after God's heart are spiritual leaders desiring to lead out of a deep relationship with God embracing the goal to get God's people to move out to where God is...being about his will, his Kingdom, and his agenda. Each chapter concludes with key points and personal questions to apply the ideas presented in the chapter. These questions are intended for personal reflection and growth, as well as for small group discussion.

My Goal

The Story Lives offers a compelling argument for missional incarnational living with a practical approach. My goal for this book is to challenge and encourage Christian leaders to step up to the plate and answer the Great Commission themselves and lead others to do the same.

This book will give leaders a simple strategy and practical suggestions to lead a missional revolution through living their own stories authentically and practically. Rather than adding more to an already full plate, this approach seeks to transform our daily lives from silos of work, school, church, and community to an integrated, organic life that demonstrates Jesus' love and provides hope and love to others.

As you read my book, I invite you to explore with me how you can tell your story and lead others to do the same. I hope you will experience God's heart through *The Story Lives*.

Chapter 1

Everyone Has A Story

One day your life will flash before your eyes.
Make sure it's worth watching.

—Author Unknown

…let the Spirit renew your thoughts and attitudes. Put on your new
nature, created to be like God—truly righteous and holy.

—Ephesians 4:23-24, NLT

Pete's Story

Almost everyone in my hometown knew me, and they either loved me or wanted nothing to do with me. Not surprising, I guess. I was that kid in town who'd put a rotting fish on my head if it got me attention. One of my less loved qualities was I'd speak first, then think. I gladly shared my opinions. A friend of mine used to rib me, saying, "Your mouth is in gear but your brain is in park." True enough.

My mouth didn't reduce my popularity. My friends liked my bravado and counted on me to be the first to try things. My personality provided me with ample character growth opportunities because I certainly suffered the consequences of my rash choices. Some of my choices left long time negative effects. Like school, I only stayed as long as required. Forget book learning; I enjoyed sports and games. People said I was smart, but I never considered myself intelligent. I learned by doing a lot of different things, but I especially liked working with my hands.

The sea and fishing is what I loved. I savored breathing in the aroma of the salty air, weathered wood, and freshly caught fish. The wind whipping against my face, the sun baking my skin, and the spray of the water against my body as I fished made any day at sea a good day. Working as a fisherman was rugged and carefree just like me. Fishing was my destiny. That's what my granddad did and what my father did. Our family's fishing operation was relatively small, nothing like those dangerous adventures of crab boats. We fished almost daily and eked out an honest living.

Most of my friends were also tough fishermen. We worked hard, had fun, and our group thrived on action and adventure. I expected to live out my days fishing hard, providing for my family, seeing my kids grow up to fish with me, and attending church. This was the way life unfolded in my town and in my family for generations. Until one day when my life was turned upside down.

I didn't see it coming, but the day I met Jesus, he changed everything. He taught a group of us on the shore, but he seemed to speak directly to me. Teaching with authority and insight, I burned with conviction from his words—words I'd never heard spoken this way before. He cast a vision for a bigger destiny. It messed with my head. I had no time for big dreams and a change of direction. What did he want from me? My course was set, and I carried a lot of responsibilities on my shoulders. This type of opportunity was for a younger man, one that still longed for more beyond life in this town. My dreams to venture out were just teenage fantasies I had buried long ago. Sure I liked to hear Jesus' teachings and strove to be a man of faith, but leaving my livelihood and responsibilities to chase after a grand vision didn't make sense. Not anymore.

Although I believed the vision Jesus cast wasn't for me, I still felt drawn to listen to him. At times, it confounded me because hanging around him wasn't comfortable on any level. Why did I stay? It's hard to say because whenever Jesus showed up, my anxiety increased and a strange sense of conviction swept over me. Normally I would have bailed. Why dwell on my past riddled with mistakes and missteps? Jesus continued to draw me even though his words seemed to highlight my shortcomings and character flaws.

I remember one time when Jesus spoke, I told him to go away. Can you imagine doing that? Well, it was vintage me! I actually said, "Just leave because I'm really no good." He heard me, but he stayed.

Jesus continually told me to think bigger. He challenged me to want more from life. I tried to tune it out because it made no sense to me. Ignoring his words worked at first, but Jesus persisted. Simply by his presence, he reawakened my yearning to make a difference. I had buried this dream so deeply that I had forgotten I'd ever embraced it in the first place. Could my life story be more than I had settled for? Should I listen to Jesus, even follow him?

One day, when I was fishing, I concluded that either Jesus was the real deal or he wasn't. He was unlike anyone else I had ever met. I could no longer ignore the obvious—Jesus was who he said he was. This life-changing realization led me to the decision to follow him, giving him my entire life. I left my life of fishing in exchange for a calling to fish for people. This decision turned my life upside down.

He repurposed my personality, experiences, and character for a greater good. He called me to spend my life reaching people and telling them all he had done for me. Jesus changed me. He transformed me from a brash, self-centered, attention seeking guy, to a leader in his movement. People even called me insightful, passionate, and humble—if that's true, the credit and praise belong to Jesus.

Some of my character transformation grew out of our crazy experiences. Just before dawn, when the other guys and I were in our boat, we saw Jesus approaching us *on* water! And it wasn't a placid lake. He came walking up amidst large, rolling waves. As an ex-fisherman, I knew the sea, and I can tell you, no one walked even on quiet waters, let alone, rough seas. Then, and I still wonder what came over me, I shouted out to Jesus, "If it's you, tell me to come."

Jesus looked directly at me, and said "Come to me."

I jumped over the side of the boat onto the water. Can you believe that? I actually walked on water! It was wild! But it didn't last long. The moment I focused on myself and the impossibility of the experience, I lost my footing and started sinking. I freaked out. I cried out to Jesus, to rescue me from drowning. Jesus saved me then justly rebuked me for my lack of faith. The experience humbled me, and it taught me to fully trust God— even when logic suggested otherwise.

Jesus is unique and amazing. I loved him and strove to bring him honor and glory. Following him, I discovered that he truly was the Son of God. He altered my life from rote and limited to transformed and filled with peace and joy. Tough times taught me these lessons. I experienced miracles, great visions, and all consuming shame. My mouth, even as Jesus' student, got me in trouble several times before I learned to fully submit all of me, including my mouth, to God.

The incident that anchored this lesson happened soon after I loudly declared that Jesus was God and the Messiah. After that great confession, my big mouth denied that I even knew Jesus. Three times! By all human accounting, I should have been disqualified for serving God. I did the unthinkable. But Jesus restored me. His forgiveness knows no bounds. After I denied him, Jesus personally forgave me and called me again to follow him. I had committed my life to following Jesus back in my hometown. Over time, I learned to fully surrender to him and let his Spirit lead me. And, I learned to use my mouth and personality to draw a crowd to introduce people to Jesus and lead them to place their faith in him.

My life played out very differently then I had imagined. I remained the guy who jumped in feet first, took chances, spoke boldly, and lived out loud. However, instead of deploying my character, strengths and life for myself, I'm glad I surrendered fully to Jesus and allowed him to transform me for his glory and the advancement of God's Kingdom.

Jesus called me to live and lead missionally—on purpose for God to spread the Good News, and incarnationally—being the hands and feet of Jesus on earth. At the end of my wild-ride of a life, I know my decision to leave the nets and follow Jesus was the right choice. I experienced the world, lived close to Jesus, sensed God's pleasure, and contributed to leading thousands of people to put their faith in Jesus. Wow! What a great life. What an amazing story! Though there were lots of challenges,

missionally—on purpose for God to spread the Good News.

hardships, and suffering, those barely compared with the great adventure, joy, and peace I experienced being in Jesus' presence and working for his

incarnationally—being the hands and feet of Jesus on earth.

Kingdom. If I could go back, I'd do it all over again. I've been with Jesus! My life counted. I fished for men and lived my story to its full potential all for the glory of God!

Jesus Transformed His Followers' Stories

No doubt you've guessed I've retold the Apostle Peter's story. His life and experiences resonate with many of us. We've all experienced some of his blunders. However, his story and life with all its doubts, bravado, faith, and failures also sets a great example for us. When our life and story belongs to Jesus, he can turn the ordinary into the extraordinary for his Kingdom. This is the reason why I retold Peter's story from my perspective to be an example of one leader's story lived on purpose. Peter chose to use his story to tell the world, his world, about Jesus. It started locally for him, but over the centuries, his story has touched people in every nation and on every continent. His life is just one story. We all have a story to tell with our lives. We all know a "Peter" or maybe we are "Peter." But his was not the only story.

If we look at the other Apostles, we see their unique approaches and personalities. John's story is very different. He also was a fisherman, who, was volatile. Jesus called him a son "of thunder," but he mellowed. Over time, his story played out as much more compliant and even gentle. In his passion for Jesus and for justice he wanted to call down fire from heaven to destroy a town, but Jesus turned this leader into a lover of God and of all people.

Then there is Nathaniel who apparently was a rule follower. As for Andrew, he brought people. Philip was persuasive. Each disciple lived a different story that fit into the overall story.

Jesus took a ragtag group of men and turned their lives upside down. He took their stories and through them changed the world—forever. He called them to join him and his story, and in his presence, he transformed them and their stories. The time they spent with him during his ministry on earth was the beginning. While on earth, he showed them his life with God. However, the true transformation of their lives and stories required the Holy Spirit rather than Jesus' physical presence.

Following his resurrection, Jesus spent time with his disciples. He instructed them to wait until the Holy Spirit came upon them. He said, "But you will receive power when the Holy Spirit comes on you; and you will be my witnesses in Jerusalem, and in all Judea and Samaria, and to the ends of the earth."[1] He told them to wait until the Holy Spirit came because they would receive power, not for their own use to glorify themselves, but to be used as witnesses for Jesus.

Jesus told them they would be witnesses to the world. Their stories that now contained three years of living with the incarnate God were to be told to the world around them. Jesus used their stories, their lives, to tell the world his story. He sent the disciples to live their lives in their current context and in their local communities. He sent them to testify to what they had seen and heard, and to show the world through the stories of their lives the truth and power of Jesus. As they lived out their transformed stories before the people, and they gave witness to the truth of Jesus in their lives, people were changed and brought to Jesus. Their stories, lived out before a watching world, transformed other people's stories. They told Jesus' story by living out the truth and transformation in their every day lives. In turn, through their witness, others found hope and purpose for their stories, and their lives were changed.

Peter stepped up as one of the key leaders in the new movement—the Church. He invested his life and sought God's leading. One day, as he and John walked to the temple to pray, a crippled beggar sat at the gate as had been his custom for years. He must have been there even when Jesus attended the temple with his disciples. Somehow, he was not one of the people Jesus chose to heal—and we know Jesus completed all the work God had sent him to do. This one was left for Peter and John. On this day, Peter and John noticed the man. They asked for his attention, and he gave it to them hoping to get some cash. Peter told him plainly, "Silver or gold I do not have, but what I have I give you. In the name of Jesus Christ of Nazareth, walk."[2] Then Peter took the man by the hand, and instantly he was healed. He jumped up and began praising God. Everyone around noticed the man, and they were amazed.

Years after he and John healed the crippled man, Peter traveled and visited the believers in Lydda. There he found a paralytic named Aeneas. He said to him, "Jesus Christ heals you. Get up and roll up your mat."[3] Instantly, Aeneas was healed. All the people of Lydda that heard of this miracle chose to believe in Jesus.

Peter lived missionally—telling the Good News, and incarnationally— being the hands and feet of Jesus. Through his witness and story people were healed and saved. The people in Joppa, near Lydda, heard Peter had arrived in town. They sent for him because a dear woman from their church had died. Peter came and prayed for God to restore Tabitha, aka Dorcas, to life. God granted his request and Tabitha was raised from the dead. Understandably, this news spread throughout Joppa, and many people believed in the Lord.

Peter lived his story and followed Jesus. He lived as a witness, telling the Good News with his life, and his words. Through his life and witness, many people believed and became Christians. For Peter it was all about Jesus.

What's Your Story?

The Bible is a story—the story of God and his people. In the Bible, "God has disclosed the shape of the story as a whole, because in Jesus the beginning and the end of the story, the alpha and the omega, are revealed, made known, disclosed."[4] Ultimately, it's all about Jesus' story.

Everyone has a story and Jesus wants to redeem each one for his glory. Only when our stories are redeemed do they take on their full potential. How about you and your story? Where are you in Jesus' story? Webster defines story in various ways. They include some of the following:

> The Bible does not tell stories that illustrate something true apart from the story.
> The Bible tells a story that is the story, the story of which our human life is a part. It is not that stories are part of human life, but that human life is part of a story.
>
> —Bishop Lesslie Newbigin

ᐸᑖ an account of incidents or events;

a statement regarding the facts pertinent to a situation in question;

a fictional narrative shorter than a novel;

the intrigue or plot of a narrative or dramatic work.

A life story is really an account of the key or notable events that make up a person's life. It can be told from various points of view. Obvious, right? Well, maybe.

We live in a world of stories. Some of the stories told around us are true and others are pure fiction. As part of God's big story being told, we each have our stories, and our stories uniquely belong to us. They are ours to tell. We're the subject matter expert. It's our story. And, we're the only ones who can decide how we tell our stories—we can choose to tell them as fiction and live a lie, or we can authentically tell them with purpose.

Each of our stories is one of a kind. But what is this significance? Why does my story, one of over 7 billion currently being "told," matter in the overall scheme of things? Maybe it only matters to me. Or, maybe my story does matter in the bigger picture. How do we know the difference? Do only famous people's stories matter? Do our stories have to be published to count? And, who decides whether our stories are significant beyond ourselves and those who deeply care about us? Over time, we may have asked ourselves one or more of these questions.

Each of our stories matters because:

We're created by God.

He handcrafted every person with a specific character and for a specific purpose.

He made us the way he intended.

He placed us in a specific time and space.

God designed us.

Each person's story is part of the bigger story—the story of God and people.

God set our stories in motion.

He invites us to tell our stories according to his plan and for his purpose. Each story is like a pixel in a picture, an elemental aspect of the whole. None of us can see the overall significance now, but each story adds to the story that God is telling. Now doesn't that give our stories an importance and urgency to be told?

The importance doesn't end there. Our stories have significance because God made each one of us, and he gave each of us our own story. And, for those of us who have accepted Jesus as our Lord and Savior, those stories have found their ultimate fulfillment, purpose, and redemption.

Our stories only take on their complete meaning and true purpose in Jesus—when they are lived for him.

How Are You Living Your Story?

You can only tell your story well if you understand it. Your story is the history of your life. You are making history as your days unfold. If you tell your story as part of God's story, you can leave a legacy by creating a worthwhile history.

All good stories have a beginning, middle and an end. A well-told story contains a plot and subplot. It often has twists and turns. In every story worth reading there is character development in the people involved.

Consider the following questions:

- How is your story playing out?
- Have you thought about your story?
- Has your life been redeemed by Jesus?
- How are you letting God shape your history?
- Has God spent time developing your character?
- Have you discovered your purpose, wiring, and God-given assignment?
- Are you living your story for God and to its full potential for ultimate Kingdom impact?

To live your story well requires intentionality. If God makes you a leader, telling your story well takes on even greater importance. It helps to understand how you're wired. When you know how God designed you, it's easier to live your story as originally intended.

Part of understanding your wiring requires:
- You know and understand your personality, strengths, character, and spiritual gifts.
- You know who you are in relation to Jesus.
- You know God's calling for you.

God grows our character as we live our story. He develops us as we experience life, make choices, endure hardships, and either suffer or rejoice in the consequences of our choices. God will lead us to deal with our fallen nature, the injuries done to our soul, and our wrong thinking. He will allow us to experience suffering to produce perseverance, character, hope, and joy. The Apostle Paul urges us to view character development as cause for joy:

> Not only that, but we rejoice in our sufferings, knowing that suffering produces endurance, and endurance produces character, and character produces hope, and hope does not put us to shame, because God's love has been poured into our hearts through the Holy Spirit who has been given to us.[5]

James understood that God uses suffering and trials to bring us to a mature faith.

> My friends, be glad, even if you have a lot of trouble. You know that you learn to endure by having your faith tested. But you must learn to endure everything, so that you will be completely mature and not lacking in anything.[6]

God allows trouble, trials, and suffering to produce great character. Only through hardship can God reveal aspects of himself. He will allow us to experience grief to get to know his comfort. He will bring us to times of need so we can experience his provision. He might allow times of powerlessness to experience his power. He gives us opportunities to wait to learn patience and experience his faithfulness. He allows tests of faith to reveal that he can be trusted in all things. The list goes on.

God longs to use all of our experiences and character growth. He desires that we invest our entire stories to tell his story. He wants his people to live as witnesses to Jesus. Through our lives and stories, he wants to demonstrate his character and great love for his people.

This book is centered on how we can use our lives and stories for greater Kingdom impact. It's dedicated to living our lives as Jesus intended—in a missional way to demonstrate Jesus' love to people around us who do not yet know him. Jesus lived his story to reveal God to his followers and bring people salvation. He invites us to do the same.

God has been in the business of teaching people about himself and a relationship with him from the beginning. As we read the stories of God's people in the Bible, we see how he teaches, using both blessing and suffering, to develop his people's character and story. God's purpose is to bring people into relationship with him and to demonstrate his love to them and through them—all to his honor and glory.

> The call to salvation is a call to be on mission with God as He reconciles a lost world to Himself through Christ. Even though you may consider yourself to be an ordinary person, God will prepare you, and then He will do His work through you, revealing Himself to a watching world.
>
> —Henry Blackaby and Claude King

Jesus also lived his story and invited others to live their stories with and for him. We have already looked at Peter and his life. Jesus explains that we were designed to have our lives make a difference. He called Peter to a higher calling than fishing. He calls us too. But what does it look like? The specifics vary for each person, but Jesus tells us that all of our stories lived for him will have an impact on the world around us.

What Is Your Story's Flavor?

One day while teaching on the mountain near the Lake of Galilee, Jesus explained that we, as God's people, are the salt of the earth. How we live our stories matters:

> You are the salt of the earth, but if salt has lost its taste, how shall its saltiness be restored? It is no longer good for anything except to be thrown out and trampled under people's feet.[7]

Salt is an important ingredient, but it has to be in the right dosage. Too much salt, and you'll ruin the food; too little and the food is bland. We, as God's people, can live lives that taste too salty, too bland, or just right. As we live our stories intentionally, we want to be the kind of salt that Jesus intended and not be too salty or too bland.

What would it look like if we were too salty? We know the taste of food when it's too salty. We know we can get thirsty.

Max—Too Salty?

Max desired to live a life of meaning and always talked about Jesus. He knew his Bible inside out and could quote from it at will. He delighted in leading the conversation to deep discussions about the application of the Bible to life issues. Unfortunately, he lacked people interpretation skills, and he failed to read social clues. Often the rest of the group sought to move on, but Max would continue. Typically people avoided hanging out with Max. He misinterpreted the situation, and he tended to judge people's motives.

A few of us who knew him, to be nice and also out of guilt, would invite him for dinner and even on some trips. These encounters would rise to the levels of an endurance contest. Max could not discern how much salt to add—either when discussing the Bible or any topic. He was too salty as a Christian. Though his topics were interesting, he always added too much. Max tried to live a life that brought flavor, preservation, and healing. He simply overdid it.

A too salty Christian might look like a regular person or there might be some tell tale signs. The person may be stiff with saltiness. The 1980's *Saturday Night Live's* portrayal of the Church Lady character illustrates what too much salt looks like to those evaluating whether to try a bite.

The world can smell the too salty Christian like ocean air—you can smell the distinct odor from far away. Yet, unlike the fresh scent of ocean air, the odor of the too salty Christian smells pungent.

When our stories are too salty, people may taste but not eat. Too salty stories may deter people from discovering the sweet flavor of Christ.

As we live our stories for Jesus, we want to maintain our flavor and do our part to be the salt of the earth. Why? So we can live stories that influence the world for good. Salt preserves, adds flavor, and disinfects. In the right quantity salt adds taste, and it enhances the distinct flavors of the food. How do we live our story? Are we at risk of coming across too salty?

Marcia—Not Salty Enough?

We desire to live with the right flavoring and aroma. We want to spread the pleasant aroma of Jesus. Neither too much nor too little salt in our stories make them effectively work. Not enough salt makes our lives bland, boring and uninspired. What would it look like if we were not salty enough? Our stories would lack truth and offer no real flavor, disinfectant, healing, or preservation. Marcia believed all the right things, but she never spoke about the importance of Jesus in her life. She provided neither flavor nor preservation.

Instead of truth, Marcia provided her presence but no hope. She was kind and helped people from the right heart motives, but God was invisible. If anyone asked her about her faith, she did not want to offend and said nothing. She knew about Jesus, God, the Bible, and prayer, but she couldn't translate any of these positive aspects of her faith for people observing her life. Her faith didn't inspire questions or passions in those who were watching her. Knowing Marcia, not having impact on people would have been the last thing she wanted to accomplish.

The world is starving for nutrition, but cannot take nourishment from a tasteless Christian. A tasteless Christian looks religious but does not provide any encouragement for people to try and sample to see if Jesus is who he says he is. When we lack salt, people also may taste but still not eat. It may present Jesus as boring and irrelevant rather than the fresh bread of life that he is.

How Salty Are You?

Since we are called to live our lives as missional people, sent out into the world to share the message of Jesus, let's evaluate how well we are living our stories being the right kind of salt of the earth. As incarnational people, let's ask if people are experiencing the love of Jesus through us.

As Christ-followers, our presence in the world should add flavor. Lives with the right saltiness will add conviction, enjoyment, and purpose to our own lives and those around us. Our lives when lived with the right amount of salt will keep things from spoiling and bring healing. We should enhance the taste and add it to the enjoyment of life.

Are we effectively salty or
have we lost our saltiness rendering us ineffective as Christians?

As we witness to Jesus' work in our lives, it's important to add the right amount of salt to a situation. Let's be appropriately salty, bringing flavor, healing, and purification. "Let your conversations be always full of grace, seasoned with salt, so that you may know how to answer everyone."[8]

Peter certainly lived an appropriately salty life. His story was interesting, brought conviction, preservation, flavor, and healing. He lived intentionally, missionally, and incarnationally. As his followers, he urges us to do the same, "Since you call on a Father who judges each man's work impartially, live your lives as strangers here in reverent fear."[9]

Consider the following questions:
- How are you doing in living out your story?
- Are you like Peter?
- How would people describe you story?
- How are you telling your story?
- Are you salty enough?
- Does your life influence the world for a Kingdom impact?

Living It Out

Your story clearly is yours to tell. God made you for a purpose. What's that purpose? How can you make your story count? How should you live your story in your neighborhood, at work, with your friends, and in the community? How is your story leading others to experience Jesus? The following pages will explore where most Christians live their stories, how Jesus lived his, and ideas for how we can live ours missionally and incarnationally. We will also explore the reasons and power of collaborating with others to tell our stories together for greater impact.

Join me on this great adventure to explore how we can more fully let our stories live!

Key Concepts

ᕤ Everyone of us has a story—each of us can only tell our own story. For us to tell the story well requires understanding who we are telling our story to and for what purpose.

ᕤ Our story matters as part of God's story. His story is one of creation and redemption. He wants to use his people to reconcile all people to himself.

ᕤ Know and tell the story. To tell the story, it's important to know and tell our story.

Questions for Living It Out

1. Where are you in Jesus' story?[10] Does your life and story belong to him?

2. Do you know your story and Jesus' call on your life? If not or for more information, visit TheStoryLives.com to find out how to discover your unique wiring.

3. Are you living out your story for yourself, your friends, or for Kingdom impact?

4. Is God working on your character? If so, how? If not, how do you perceive the condition of your character?

5. What's your salt content?

6. Where are you living your story?

Notes

1. Acts 1:8, NIV

2. Acts 3:6, NIV

3. Acts 9:34, NIV

4. Lesslie Newbigin, *The Open Secret: An Introduction to the Theology of Mission* (Grand Rapids, MI: Wm. B. Eerdmans Publishing Company, 1995), 85.

5. Romans 5:3-5, ESV

6. James 1:2-3, CEV

7. Matthew 5:13-14, ESV

8. Colossians 4:6, NIV

9. 1 Peter 1:17, NIV

10. If you have not yet joined Jesus' story and would like to know more, contact the author at henriet@thestorylives.com.

Chapter 2

Stories Lived in Boxes

Go and preach the good news to everyone in the world.

—Mark 16:15, CEV

Do all the good you can by all the means you can in all the places you can at all the times you can to all the people you can as long as ever you can.

—John Wesley

He who has an ear, let him hear what the Spirit says to the churches.

—Revelation 3:22, NIV

John's Story

As an entrepreneur and CEO of a small manufacturing business, John Mortins knew a small taste of success. His life philosophy was steeped in his belief that if God blessed you—liberally share it with others. He generously donated, but giving money left him unfulfilled. He longed for meaningful involvement.

He and his wife, Anne, had participated in ministries and activities at their previous church. John had learned that his options were limited: teach Sunday school, work in youth ministry, lead a small group, usher, or do parking lot duty. He had tried most of them because he believed you serve God through ministries at church, but these options left him dissatisfied. God made him an entrepreneur, excellent at strategic planning, and running an organization. He had offered his services to the senior pastor who had encouraged him and invited him to his own small group, but the pastor hadn't accepted his help and expertise in leadership or operations at or beyond the church.

John also had tried to volunteer in the community, although he didn't believe this was truly serving God. To his chagrin, the choices there were not much better. They seemed limited to mundane tasks like stocking shelves and weeding parks. John attempted to give back in other ways. He had provided his office for community meetings. He had lent his trucks to various nonprofits. He had even used his cabin to give people retreat opportunities. None of it fulfilled him. He wanted to serve God in a way that made an impact and used his talents.

His electronic calendar pinged, reminding him of his lunch meeting with Brandon Willis. *It's that guy from City Community Church Anne and I met a few Sundays ago when we first started going there.* Brandon had seemed eager to talk to him and wanted to take him to lunch. *Brandon is another CEO and owner of his own furniture company—might be a good contact.*

Close to noon, John arrived at the restaurant. Brandon greeted him with the same enthusiasm John had noticed that Sunday. They were seated, ordered, and exchanged the usual small talk. John learned that Brandon had attended City Community for years.

"We started attending City Community a few months ago." John smiled. "I'm glad we ran into each other at church."

"Do you know how easy it is to go to church every Sunday and never meet people?" Brandon shook his head and laughed.

"I think this is the way it is in most churches. Warm the pew for an hour and then run to the parking lot." John smirked. "I think some people try to beat the land speed record to get on the road the minute the pastor says, 'Amen.'"

Brandon mentioned he had tried to volunteer at previous churches and even in the ministries at City Community. "One Easter, I was assigned the lower parking lot duty and ended up standing in the bushes wearing my best suit!"

John laughed, knowing this type of scenario by heart.

Brandon asked if John was plugged into ministry anywhere. John explained how he had tried without finding his fit, "I want to serve God, but I don't know how to do it at church. I feel guilty about volunteering outside the church. And even there, I've not found my niche." John shrugged. "Am I just supposed to make money and give it away?"

Brandon leaned forward across the table, "John, I want to tell you about a new way of serving I've discovered thanks to a local nonprofit." He cocked his head and added, "This was my ulterior motive for asking you, a fellow business executive, to lunch."

John raised his eyebrows, unsure where this was headed.

Brandon smiled and continued, "This nonprofit partners with churches and other nonprofits to provide opportunities for executives, professionals and business people to use their gifts and skills to impact the community for Christ. They recognized there's usually no place for professionals, executives, and leaders to serve in the community or in churches."

"Tell me more." John put down his fork to focus on what Brandon was saying.

"There are many business people making significant contributions and spreading the Gospel through meaningful service." Brandon cleared his throat, "I'm involved in helping a local nonprofit create a business plan to improve efficiencies, streamline operations, and increase visibility. I particularly noted they hadn't developed a clear, concise statement about who they were as an organization." Brandon smiled. "I told them that if I woke them up in the middle of the night and trout-slapped them, they all should be giving me the same answer. It's been great to help them even with their slow progress, and I'm finally doing something useful."

"You've got my full attention now," John said.

"I donate a couple of hours a week. It's not a Christian nonprofit, but they know that I'm a Christian. Some have asked me about my faith. When they do, I speak to them in plain English and answer their questions." Brandon hesitated as if he was checking to see if John was tracking with him. "Mostly I try to demonstrate Jesus to them through my actions. Through my involvement, I've learned that the best way to share the Gospel is to live, act, and *be* Jesus to those we work with. Even then, I only take it as far as their questions lead me."

John waited as he could see Brandon was collecting his thoughts.

Brandon continued, "Through studying the Scriptures, I'm convinced that it's up to God to draw people to himself. We need to be willing, ready, and trained to be witnesses if he opens the opportunities, but it's not up to us to make it happen." Brandon pinched his lips. "Sometimes it's tough for a guy who lives to, 'make it happen.'"

As John drove back to his office, he mulled over their conversation. That guy was serving in the community and making his faith count. *I wish I knew of an opportunity like that.* Yet, as soon as he returned to his office, the work pulled him out of his missional daydream.

After a full day, John was ready to call it a night, but he knew Anne wanted to talk. He suspected she'd been praying for him to find some Christian guys to do stuff with. He told her briefly about the conversation, and she smiled in her knowing way.

Anne said, "What Brandon is doing is what you've been talking about for the last few years. Why don't you look for an opportunity like that?"

On Sunday, John asked Brandon to keep an eye out for a business type opportunity at a local nonprofit. He figured that'd buy him some time since he hadn't totally wrapped his mind around the situation.

One morning, a few weeks later, he received an email about an opportunity that might fit what he was looking for. It was a local teen hangout center called Jonathan House. They needed help organizing and running operations. That's what he loved to do. He responded to the email and scheduled a meeting with the director. They hit it off, and she gave him the freedom to do what he was made to do. He committed to volunteering one morning a week.

John also joined Brandon's group of CEOs that were part of a local missional leader network. They met monthly, shared stories, prayed together, and exchanged ideas. This was rewarding, connecting with other executives who did similar stuff.

After a few months, his business was moving to the next level. He knew God blessed him, maybe in part because he was investing his life for God's Kingdom. He now donated his time and his money.

John and Brandon met on a regular basis. "Brandon, the bottom line is that for the first time I'm serving God and loving it. I'm living my life and my story out in the world. Every time I volunteer at Jonathan House, I get an opportunity to show the love of Jesus. Sometimes I get to share about my beliefs. No one ever asked me about my faith before. Now it's natural, and I feel comfortable sharing."

Brandon smiled and nodded. "That was my experience too. Instead of figuring out how to share Jesus like I'd been taught, I now live it. Talking about my faith flows out of my life."

They both marveled how living their stories out loud was fun and the easiest way to share Jesus. Who knew?

Your Story Is Unique

Everyone has a story and each of our stories is unique to us. There are no repeats. Each story contributes to the bigger story of God the Creator and his creation. Our stories matter.

It seems that if God went through the effort to make each of us a unique creation, and he did not hit the copy button to run off a batch of Susan's or a cluster of Bob's, he surely had a purpose. God designed each of us exactly the way he intended for this time and place. Imagine that! We are specially designed for our local and current circumstances, including our family, friends, and community.

Your story is unlike any other ever told. Sure there are some similarities and recurrent themes throughout people's stories, but there are no reprints. Your story fits in your family and community unlike any other story ever told. That leads to some important questions: Who knows your story? Where do you live your story? Who sees it and hears it? Who is meant to see it and hear it? Why did God design your story the way it is? What did he craft your story to be about and why?

God Has a Plan for Each of Us!

God carefully created you and me with details and specifics. As the Apostle Paul tells us God, "chose us in him (Jesus) before the creation of the world."[1] Why did he choose us? He chose us to be "holy and blameless in his sight." He adopted us, and he had a plan for us "in accordance with his pleasure and will." Why? "To the praise of his glorious grace." He even told us what his ultimate will is that he "purposed in Christ."[2] His ultimate plan is to bring all things in heaven and on earth together under Jesus.

To highlight:

- Our stories are specifically designed to fit into God's overall plan.

- They're designed to be lived in such a way that they bring praise and glory to God.

- They fit into God's purpose to bring all things together under Jesus' reign.

That is awesome, don't you think?

I imagine serious Christ-followers will be nodding their heads in agreement. Of course, our stories are unique. Of course, we are called to live them out in our community. These truths makes sense. Based on Ephesians 1, we believe we are chosen! We like being chosen. *God knew and chose me, the individual, before he made the world. That's great. I am special to God.* We love this thought!

But hold on. Do we believe we are individually chosen for individual blessings? Or, do we see ourselves as part of God's overall plan? The Bible tells us we are chosen:

- for a purpose beyond ourselves;

- as part of God's overall plan; and

- to be witnesses and to spread the Good News.

This is bigger than our own story. As Christ-followers, we are all chosen, and we each have a story to tell—not for our self-interest but for God's glory. Our job entails living our stories and telling them for God's purpose as he calls and directs us. Where do we live our stories?

Who Knows Your Story?

Most of us, as we progress in the Christian life, have chosen to belong to a local church, attend Sunday morning services, and possibly a small group. We may serve in one or more of the ministries at the church, we have a regular quiet time that includes reading and studying the Bible, and we pray. These are all worthwhile and honorable things belonging to a life of faith.

Now look around in your life. Who knows your story? Where do we as Christians tell our stories? Many of us spend our time outside of work, school, and our families, relating to people at church! We live our stories in the confines of our local church and with the people there. They are our friends online. We go to small group with them. We do ministry with them. Many of us live inside a Christian bubble!

If, as Christians, we only live our stories with other Christians, how will our stories contribute to God's purpose of bringing all things in heaven and on earth together under Jesus? Before you quit reading and decide that this is all too much or you think I have forgotten part of Scripture, hang on. Of course we are admonished not to "give up meeting together, as some are in the habit of doing."[3] It's clear in the New Testament that the church met regularly. People were to share their lives with other believers and be there for each other. In Acts 2, we learn that the believers gathered daily and spent time together.

In his last prayer, Jesus talks about the fact that his followers are not of the world anymore than he is of the world.[4] God tells us to gather...but he also calls us to be among our neighbors.

Live "Out Loud"

Who knows your story? If our stories are going to be used, they need to be lived "out loud." For people to know our stories, they have to see them or hear them. This does not mean we have to go on talk shows, write a book, or broadcast our stories to the world. Not everyone needs to know each of our stories, only the right people. The right people that God intended to be touched by our stories are the ones to:

- Hear it;
- Read it;
- See it.

It's key to God's plan that people see our life stories played out in order for these stories to be used by God to help people make sense of their lives, and to lead them to be an integral part of God's overall plan and purpose.

Who are the right people? I believe they are the people that God has already placed in our lives. It probably includes our family, our friends, our community, people at school, colleagues at work, shopkeepers and waiters at the places we frequent, our neighbors and anyone else God might set on our paths.

That seems like we might have to relate to many people. Who has time? Don't panic.

We can be confident God doesn't intend us to tell our complete life stories to each person we encounter. That would require more time than any one of us has. And, most of the people in our sphere probably aren't up for a coffee or lunch appointment to hear every last detail of our stories. Let's live our everyday lives in such a way people can "read" our stories by the way we:

- respond;
- act;
- love; and
- speak.

The Early Church Told a Story

The early church lived "out loud" in a way that brought many people to faith. How did they do it? Jesus instructed his disciples that life in the Kingdom of God revolved around love for God and love for each other. Scot McKnight, New Testament scholar, calls it the "Jesus Creed," which involves loving God and loving others—Jesus' intent for the Church. McKnight writes, "…it's the Jesus Creed ultimately that is the design of God for our lives. We are made to love God by following Jesus and to love others."[5] God's people—the Church—were to love one another as Jesus had loved them. When the believers lived out this life of love, it would testify to the truth of Jesus and the message of the Good News. The early church lived that out as recorded in Acts 2 and 4. Love distinguished the believers from the world around them.

In his writings, the Apostle John shared the importance of love. He writes, "This is the message you heard from the beginning: We should love one another…. This is how we know what love is: Jesus Christ laid down his life for us. And we ought to lay down our lives for our brothers."[6]

They Lived a Story of Love Together

The disciples and the people in the early church loved each other as Jesus taught them. They shared their lives and their goods. They spent time together on a daily basis. Believers also went to the temple courts as part of their daily prayers. Living a life of faith together was part of their daily practice. They lived life together in a visible way for the world around them to see.

> They devoted themselves to the apostles' teaching and to the fellowship, to the breaking of bread and to prayer. … All the believers were together and had everything in common. Selling their possessions and goods, they gave to anyone as he had need. Every day they continued to meet together in the temple courts. They broke bread in their homes and ate together with glad and sincere hearts, praising God and enjoying the favor of all the people. And the Lord added to their number daily those who were being saved.[7]

Jesus told the Apostles to live a life of love. And, we can see the results. God added to their number daily! Sometimes, he added thousands of people at a time. Clearly, the Apostles and believers demonstrated their faith to those around them. They didn't just separately gather in homes or buildings. They didn't hide away. After Pentecost, the Apostles continued going to the temple to pray. They also preached and taught in Solomon's Colonnade as recorded in Acts 3. People in the community saw how the Church lived and heard the messages the Apostles taught. The way they lived their lives, and how they showed their love for each other testified to the truth of their words.

They Visibly Gathered as God's People

Most likely, the New Testament church did not gather in big buildings with people facing forward and listening to a professional pastor teaching from a stage or pulpit. As the Gospel spread and more people became followers of Jesus, people seemed to have met together in various places. Neither Jesus nor the Apostles nor Paul prescribe a certain place for meeting together. Paul met with worshipers of God by the river in Philippi. After Lydia became a Christian, the "church" met at her house.[8] Paul greets the church that meets at Priscilla and Aquila's house as recorded in Romans 16. There are other references Paul makes to the church—the gathered Christians—meeting at someone's house. Not all churches necessarily met in homes, but they gathered, both publicly and in homes, in a way that lived out their stories. After all, people were added to the Church daily—this could only happen if people could see their stories lived out.

The church was the gathering of believers. It was the *ekklesia*, or called out ones, an assembly of citizens.[9] In this case, they were the assembled citizens of the new Kingdom. The disciples continued meeting together in the name of Jesus. Meeting together in Jesus' name is what "church" signifies.[10]

They gathered as a people, as the family of God, and they shared life together. They devoted themselves to the Apostles' teaching. The community of faith took it upon themselves to know and live the teachings that were passed down. They focused on Jesus' teachings as taught by the Apostles. They prayed. They worshipped. They shared meals. They shared possessions and goods. They lived out their faith. They told their stories together for the world around them to see and experience.

Today's Church Tells a Different Story

Our current churches often create a different picture and experience than what we see in Acts. In many cases, our churches resemble more of a manufactured reality. It's not daily life, but a church culture. Authors, George Barna and Frank Viola put it this way, "Strikingly, much of what we do for 'church' was lifted directly out of pagan culture in the postapostolic period."[11] They say that our current Sunday morning church practices didn't come from Jesus or the early Church. According to Barna and Viola, much of what Christians today embrace as church and worship came from pagan culture and was incorporated after the Apostles died, starting as early as the middle of the first millennium, and it has continued throughout the Church age.

> God is about a big purpose in and for the whole creation. The church has been called into life to be both the means of this mission and a foretaste of where God is inviting all creation to go. Just as its Lord is a mission-shaped God, so the community of God's people exists, not for themselves but for the sake of the work. Mission is therefore not a program or project some people in the church do from time to time...; the church's very nature is to be God's missionary people.
>
> —Alan Roxburgh and Fred Romanuk

Are We Going to Church or Being the Church?

Now, most of us *go* to church and *work* in ministries and activities *at* church. We attend small groups with people from church that often are folks we do not really do life with—at least, this is true for most people in small groups most of the time. It's a church reality that seems normal to people in church, but it's not natural for those in the community around us.

To reach the community, many churches try various programs to attract people to the church. Of course, many of these activities are good. Some churches have unique approaches. Some have grown very large. Several of these mega churches publish their approaches as a guide to doing church well—which to those who seek to emulate their practices primarily means getting more people to attend services and ministries. Pastor Steven Furtick[12] calls it "Mr. Potato Head church" where pastors and leaders take an ear from this model of doing church, an eye from another, a foot from another, etc. These parts are then assembled to create their own version of church.

There isn't anything wrong with learning from other approaches as long as God is leading the approach for each church. What about our church? Are we doing Mr. Potato Head church? Is the Mr. Potato Head church model motivated to honor God or to attract more people and cash? Are we *being* the church, living out our faith in love, or are we *going* to church?

Trying to create a "church experience" that draws many people to get the numbers up seems not to have been the way of the New Testament church. There were lots of numbers in Acts with 3,000 and 5,000 being added on different occasions. But these numbers were not added to one or other local expression of church. They were added to the Church, the *ekklesia*, the people of God, because people saw the way they lived and wanted to be part of the called out ones, *ekklesia*. They joined the Church even though there was a cost…sometimes they paid with their lives as a result of being part of the church.

Do We Tell Stories about Programs or People?

Today many Christians live as "consumers of religious goods and services"[13] instead of disciples who live out their stories in the community for God's purpose and glory. As consumers of religious goods and services, we're not a contrast society, but we look like a religious version of our neighbors with the same problems and challenges. We struggle like everyone else without hope, love, and joy to offer. If we're only religious consumers without stories that tell of God's goodness and draw others to Jesus, what are we doing? This condition has led to disillusionment with church and Christianity, leading many to ask, "What is the church? Is it a building? A set of programs?" But was that Jesus' idea and call for the church?

According to George Barna, author and researcher, millions of Christians no longer attend church although they still believe in and follow Jesus.[14] These disillusioned Christians have left the church. They are seeking an authentic expression of church rather than what they believe to be a collection of programs or attending a performance in a building.

Now you may ask, "Don't churches do evangelism and try to reach the community?" Many do. My question to the church is, "Does it work?" According to Brad Smith, president of Bakke Graduate University of Ministry, the evangelistic approach of churches has "Christians acquiring experiences"—evangelistic experiences. Those who go on short-term or long-term missions may spiritually grow, but their efforts may not translate to truly reaching people with the love of Jesus. Do people who do not yet know him come to know him through these mission events? Are they moving closer to a relationship with Jesus? Smith concluded that it takes "people to go and be…to live as witnesses. It's all about Jesus."[15] Only living as witnesses moves people closer to a relationship with Jesus. We need to help people live out their stories as witnesses—as part of our every day lives. Living our stories will help the church, the called out ones, to connect with where God is at work in the community.

As Christians, we often live our stories inside the church and its programs…only. These expressions of church might not help us to tell our stories in a way that leads people to Jesus.

How will the world know of God's love for them?

How will people come to know who Jesus really is?

Personally knowing God's love and living it out, outside the church walls, is the answer to these questions. Let's know, *really* know, Jesus in order to demonstrate who he is to others.

Church in a Box

According to Jesus, the Church is his body made up of believers. It's a living and breathing organism. The Church cannot be contained or trapped in a box.

Years ago, I heard, Reggie McNeal, missional leadership specialist, refer to our current churches as box churches.[16] I have come to think of them as church done in a box. When we attend church in the box then our stories tend to be lived in the box. These stories may be wonderful and worthwhile. In fact, we may be doing great good through volunteering "at church," but who knows our story? Who sees it? I believe Jesus sent us to live beyond the box.

I confess that before hearing Reggie McNeal explain how to think differently, my view was too small. I lived in the box. I served as pastor of adult ministries of a church of 1100 people, of which 600 to 700 were adults. My responsibilities included small groups, pastoral care, local missional engagement, as well as the men's and women's ministries. Our desire as a church and my personal passion was to have a missional mindset and approach. Our goal was to be the church, grow disciples, and reach out to those who were not yet followers of Jesus. We tried to engage the community and be involved outside the walls of the church. Sounds good, right? Maybe.

My vision was too small. I viewed outreach through the lens of our local church. Frankly, it really was about reaching people to come to church. I had fallen into the trap that theologian and author, David Bosch, shares, evangelization is trying to "re-recruit people" into the church instead of back to God.[17]

We engaged people through our missional programs and expressions. We touched the community through our people and ministries. Why? Ultimately, so that people would come to Jesus, but also so they'd come to our church. After all, for pastors and volunteers there is the pressure to grow the church...the local expression of church in the building. In the end, it was about the box and not the Kingdom. I didn't realize my priorities had shifted because my desire was to serve Jesus and to bring people into relationship with him. In reality, I was competing for people to come to my church...to the box. My story remained tied to the box.

Live Beyond the Box

To follow Jesus requires us to live our stories beyond the box! Jesus in his prayer recorded in John 17 prays for all believers. He asks his Father, "My prayer is not that you take them out of the world but that you protect them from the evil one. They are not of the world, even as I am not of it. Sanctify them by the truth; your word is truth. As you sent me into the world, I have sent them into the world."[18]

Jesus prayed for his followers to be protected as they lived in the world. He sent them, and us, out as his witnesses. "And you will be my witnesses in Jerusalem, and in all Judea and Samaria, and to the ends of the earth."[19]

Church Outside the Box

According to author and pastor, Leonard Sweet, God is always up to something. At a pastors' gathering, he asked us, "Do you know God well enough to know what God is up to?"[20] An interesting question to ask pastors. Do we?

If God is up to something all the time, and we want to be part of what he is doing in the world, then it behooves us to know him well enough so we can join him. It seems that one place that God is at work is in the church. In fact, according to Sweet, God is rebooting the church. Instead of worrying about attendance, buildings and cash, it's important the church of the twenty-first century focuses on God and on people. He claims the church needs to redefine itself into a missional community.

Love in Action: Missional, Relational and Incarnational

What does that mean? Sweet discussed three things: missional, relational, and incarnational. Missional implies action, requiring us to intentionally focus on going out to be with people. Relational entails being with people in a way that mirrors God who exists in and for relationship. And, incarnational, in essence, refers to living out Jesus' love to others in tangible ways unique to the situation and environment. In summary, Sweet told the gathered pastors: the church needs to help people live and tell their stories…beyond the box.

Our assignment is to get out there and love people—with actions demonstrating Jesus' love. Pastor Miles McPherson put it more bluntly. He said what we need is, "Not butts in the seats but butts in the streets."[21] Churches have taught their people to come and sit, not go and serve! Let's reverse this. Let's tell our stories! As God's people, let's tell our stories in a way they can be heard—through love in action by the power of the Holy Spirit.

> A missional church is a church that is shaped by participating in God's mission, which is to set things right in a broken, sinful world, to redeem it, and to restore it to what God has always intended for the world.
>
> —Lois Barrett, Darrell Guder, and Walter Hobbs.

When Jesus was about to leave this earth to return to his Father, he told his disciples to wait for the Holy Spirit.[22] Why? Because they would be his witnesses, and they needed his Spirit and power to accomplish that. Witness to what? To the love of Jesus. We need the Spirit like they did… perhaps even more!

When we live our stories like Jesus lived his, people can experience his love through us. He knew that living our stories to spread his love and bring glory to God requires the power and love of the Spirit. We cannot go it alone. We need the Holy Spirit's help. As missionary and theologian, Bishop J.E. Lesslie Newbigin, put it, "Because the Spirit himself is sovereign over the mission, the church can only be the attentive servant. In sober truth the Spirit is himself the witness who goes before the church in its missionary journey… . The church is witness insofar as it follows obediently where the Spirit leads."[23] The Holy Spirit will help us live out our stories as witnesses of who Jesus is and what he has done.

We need to take our stories to people in our community. We live in a post-Christian culture where people are not drawn to Christianity.[24] Most people who do not know Jesus aren't going to come to church! They will not look for God in church. We need to go to them. Brandon and John took their stories outside the church, and they lived their faith in the community. They visibly and effectively served, living, and telling Jesus' story.

Living It Out

Many Christians live their stories in boxes. If we stay in these church boxes, people in our community won't hear our stories. For our stories to have the desired effect, let's get out of the box. People are hungry for the love and truth of Jesus. On Sunday when we gather, if that's when we gather, it ought to be a celebration of what God is doing through us in our communities. If we live our stories and people see Jesus' love in action, we're able to bring God genuine worship for what he has done in and through us. Our gatherings should bring him our worship and our offerings of our lives, our money, and our praise.

"But thanks be to God, who always leads us in triumphal procession in Christ and through us spreads everywhere the fragrance of the knowledge of him."[25]

Key Concepts

ᴄ☞ Everyone has a story to tell as part of God's bigger story.

ᴄ☞ Our stories are to be lived out in the community God placed us in. We are his witnesses.

ᴄ☞ Many Christians live their stories in boxes.

ᴄ☞ It's important to get out of the box and live our stories out loud.

Questions for Living It Out

1. Everyone has a story. Do you know the point of your story, and how it relates to the big story God desires to tell? Do you really know Jesus?

2. Who knows your story? Where do you live your story? Who sees it and hears it? Who is meant to see it and hear it?

3. Why did God make your story the way it is? What did he craft your story to be about and why?

4. Do you believe that we are individually chosen for individual blessings? Or, do you see yourself as part of God's overall plan? Do you realize that you were chosen for a purpose beyond yourself?

5. Is your vision big enough? Are you thinking about your church or God's Kingdom?

6. Is your story tied to the church 'box' or are you a witness in the community for Jesus, demonstrating who he is and what he has done?

Notes

1. Ephesians 1:4, NIV

2. Ephesians 1:4-9, NIV

3. Hebrews 10:25, NIV

4. See John 17:14

5. Scot McKnight, *The Jesus Creed: Loving God, Loving Others* (Brewster, MA: Paraclete Press, 2004), 22.

6. 1 John 3:11, 16, NIV

7. Acts 2:42, 44-47, NIV

8. See Acts 16

9. Liddell and Scott define *ekklesia* as "an assembly of citizens summoned by the crier, the legislative assembly." Henry G. Liddell and Robert Scott, *A Greek-English Lexicon* (New York: Oxford University Press, 1992), 206.

10. Joel B. Green, Scot McKnight, and I. Howard Marshall, *Dictionary of Jesus and the Gospels* (Downers Grove, IL: InterVarsity Press, 1992), 122.

11. Frank Viola and George Barna, *Pagan Christianity?: Exploring the Roots of Our Church Practices* (Carol Stream, IL: Tyndale House Publishers, 2008), 6.

12. Furtick, Steven, Lead pastor of Elevation Church in Charlotte, NC. Nov. 2009. National Outreach Convention, San Diego, CA.

13. Smith, Brad. Nov. 2009. C*ity Signals: Connecting Service to True Outreach & Growth*. National Outreach Convention, San Diego, CA.

14. George Barna, *Revolution* (Carol Stream, IL: Tyndale House Publishers, 2005), 11.

15. Smith, Brad. Nov. 2009. C*ity Signals: Connecting Service to True Outreach & Growth*. National Outreach Convention, San Diego, CA.

16. Reggie McNeal, Warm Beach Camp, November 2006.

17. David J. Bosch, *Believing in the Future: Toward a Missiology of Western Culture* (Valley Forge, PA: Trinity Press International, 1995), 30.

18. John 17:15-18, NIV

19. Acts 1:8, NIV

20. Leonard Sweet, Free Methodist Pastors Day, October 8, 2008. Redmond, Washington.

21. McPherson, Miles. Nov. 2009. *Leading a Church into the Community*. National Outreach Convention, San Diego, CA.

22. See Acts 1:8

23. Lesslie Newbigin, *The Open Secret: An Introduction to the Theology of Mission* (Grand Rapids, MI: Wm. B. Eerdmans Publishing Company, 1995), 61.

24. Smith, Brad. Nov. 2009. C*ity Signals: Connecting Service to True Outreach & Growth*. National Outreach Convention, San Diego, CA.

25. 2 Corinthians 2:14, NIV

Chapter 3

Observing Jesus' Story

*Christ was truly God. But he did not try to remain equal with God.
Instead he gave up everything and became a slave, when he became like one
of us. Christ was humble. He obeyed God and even died on a cross. Then God
gave Christ the highest place and honored his name above all others. So at the
name of Jesus everyone will bow down, those in heaven, on earth, and under
the earth. And to the glory of God the Father everyone will openly agree,
'Jesus Christ is Lord!'*

—Philippians 2:6-11, CEV

The Miracle Meal Story

His cousin's death hit the teacher hard. He longed for time alone to process
his loss. Events in his life and ministry were taking their toll on his strength
and endurance. The word "busy" understated the activity level in his life. He
spent long hours with people healing, teaching and preaching to them. His
schedule left little time to be by himself, and now he deeply craved solitude.
The teacher needed to spend time alone with God.

After his last appointment, he had slipped away with his closest friends,
his students—they needed rest too. They sailed to an out-of-the-way place.
But some people were vigilant in seeking him and had spotted him from
the shore. He had always strived to avoid celebrity status and attention,
but people followed him wherever he traveled. This time was no exception.

Soon after they moored the boat and walked to their remote getaway, people started arriving at the same place. Men, women, and children walked from nearby villages, and many had traveled a long time to see him. Although he sought solitude to recharge and grieve his cousin's death, the needs of the crowd touched his heart, and he realized God had other plans for his time. He faithfully surrendered to God's will, and chose to set aside his own needs for now, in order to serve those who had followed him with such childlike faith.

Thousands of people streamed across the hillside, finding places to sit and wait. They sought his presence for hope and healing. The teacher's heart filled with care and compassion for them. He chose to heal their sick. It took a long time and dusk fell across the sky. He barely noticed the day was drawing to a close. His students approached him, and urged him to send the people away to nearby towns before nightfall. They told him, "Teacher, dismiss all these people so they can get to the villages before dark and have dinner."

The teacher smiled. He recognized this situation as a great opportunity to demonstrate God's love and power. He also wanted to test his students. He told them, "We don't need to send them away. Why don't you guys feed them?"

One student's eyes widened in disbelief, and anxiously said, "How can we do that? It would take a full year's salary."

Pointing to a little boy nearby, another student haltingly suggested, "All we have is some bread and some fish."

"Perfect. Bring those to me." The teacher instructed his students to have people sit on the grass. He took the bread and fish, thanked God, broke the bread, and gave it to his students to distribute.

As they obeyed, they were amazed at what happened. They walked amongst the people, up and down the hillside, and observed how the small amount of food turned into a gigantic meal feeding over five thousand people. Finally, the students returned baskets brimming with leftovers.

"I've never had this experience before, but it doesn't surprise me!" One student said laughing.

Another student pumped the air in excitement, "Our teacher is amazing! How does he do these extraordinary things on a regular basis?"

They marveled at the incredible journey they were on with him. The teacher loved people. He healed them, cared for them, and now he fed them. The students experienced this same love. He always taught them even though he often caught them off-guard and unprepared.

The teacher felt satisfied. What a great day it had been, but now he needed to spend the evening alone. He told his students and the crowd to leave. He stayed behind and climbed a mountain to finally be by himself. All he could do now, all he wanted to do, was pray. He needed God to restore him, comfort him, and be with him. He needed God's refreshing presence to face the next day, and to be renewed and strengthened for the upcoming events. There would be more people to teach and serve.

He Prepared for His Future Calling

I love the story of Jesus and his disciples feeding the 5000. It clearly shows who Jesus is—his compassion, his love for people, and his power. It also shows that he was truly human with the frailties and challenges of life. We can learn about Jesus when we examine Scripture and study the context beyond the recorded words. The Gospels tell the story with a purpose, but they are not written like memoirs with all the details we might wish to read.

We basically know very little about Jesus' life. We've been given a few chapters about his birth and early years, and the remainder of the Gospels tells us about his last three years of life on earth. Most of the chapters focus on the last few weeks of his 33 years. Yet, the Apostle John[1] says if everything were written down that Jesus did, the accounts would be endless.

His disciples probably only knew him for the last three years of his life. Luke and Mark, two of the authors of the Gospels, knew mostly about Jesus through others, research, or by following him as part of the church after his death and resurrection. Luke might have never met him. Yet both of them have given us a written account of Jesus' story.

Based on the Scriptures, we know Jesus was there when the world was made. He spoke it into being.[2] This world, his world, was hijacked by sin and evil. God the Father decided to send his Son, Jesus—the Word—to redeem his creation. God the Son became God in man—God incarnate. Jesus chose to surrender all to redeem the creation he was part of originating.

God desires reconciliation—he wants to reconcile humankind to himself. To accomplish his goal of reconciliation, he sent Jesus. God doesn't need to be reconciled to people. We, every person God created, are the ones who need to be reconciled to God. It takes a Savior. God desires this reconciliation, and he initiated it by sending Jesus into a little body—a baby boy—to grow up, to be a sinless toddler, young boy, youth, and adult.

For the first thirty years, Jesus lived his story in obscurity. Based on the Scriptures, we know he was a good son. He never sinned. The only information about him, besides his peculiar birth and dramatic flight to safety, is his appearance in the temple when he was twelve years old. It would be close to the time of the Jewish Bar Mitzvah, which happens at age of thirteen, at which time, he would become obligated to observe the Law of Moses and the commandments. At this exact time, Jesus chose to be with his Father. Not Joseph, but his heavenly Father. He apparently knew that God was his real Father. His earthly parents were confused and angry. Yet Jesus knew what he needed to do. We know that despite his parents' confusion, he did not sin, even if they were worried and searching for him.

After this incident, we know nothing about Jesus' next 18 years. He probably lived a normal life maturing, experiencing community and family, learning the Scriptures, seeing his people, and dealing with the Roman oppression. He lived in a community and in a specific cultural environment. Then when he turned 30, the age that learned men had the authority to teach others, Jesus, the rabbi (teacher), appeared on the scene. Did he study under a rabbi? How did he become learned? We don't know the answers.

What we do know is that Jesus fulfilled the promises in Scripture made about him. When he appeared, he entered on the path prepared for him by John the Baptist. People were coming to John looking for the Kingdom of God. Before John the Baptist arrived, God had been silent for about 400 years. People were hungry for a word from the Lord. They came to hear John preach about repentance. Many were baptized. In the middle of this scene, Jesus walked up. John pointed out that Jesus was the Lamb of God; the one he had been talking about. John testified that Jesus was the one they were waiting for. On Jesus' insistence, John baptized him.

Jesus started his public ministry with a public baptism. John had been at the Jordan River talking about Jesus and baptizing scores of people for repentance. Jesus did not need to repent, but he did need to be baptized because he'd come to earth as a man to set people free. To accomplish this, he needed to become one of us. He fully identified with the people he came to redeem.

At Jesus' baptism, the glory of the Trinity—God the Father, God the Son, and God the Holy Spirit—appeared. As Jesus rose from the water, God the Spirit descended on him in the form of a dove, and God the Father spoke, and said, "This is my Son, whom I love; with him I am well pleased."[3]

What an amazing time in human history! The Triune God appeared as Jesus began his ministry on earth—the ministry of reconciliation. He came to reconcile people to God. God punctuated this assignment at the start of Jesus' ministry by showing up and approving of Jesus. From that moment on, Jesus lived on earth out of approval, following God's leading. He looked to his Father for guidance and strength.

Jesus said with full authority, "I do not act on my own, but only as I've heard and observed from my Father."[4]

After the momentous occasion of his baptism, the Spirit led Jesus into the desert to be tested. Following 40 days of fasting, Satan arrived on the scene to tempt him. Jesus passed three tests—making food, worshipping Satan, and testing God—thrown at him by Satan, and then he set off on his public ministry.

He Lived Out His Story

Jesus lived as a rabbi. He chose twelve disciples and had many other followers. He lived with them. He traveled around Israel and nearby areas. He showed great love for the people and taught them about God. People had lived without a word from God for so long, but Jesus now reminded

> 'Who is Jesus?'
> He is the Son, sent by the Father
> and anointed by the Spirit
> to be the bearer of
> God's kingdom to the nations.
>
> —Bishop Lesslie Newbigin

them of the promises and lived out his story as God's Son sent to bring hope, the Good News, and peace. He came to bring life and freedom. He came to bring about the Kingdom of God here on earth.

His message was clear: "The Kingdom of Heaven is near."[5] How could people tell the Kingdom of Heaven was near? Well, they knew from the book of Isaiah—the Kingdom of God would have a certain look and feel. The signs would be obvious:

- The eyes of the blind will be opened.
- The ears of the deaf unstopped.
- The lame will leap like a deer.
- The mute will talk.[6]

He Opened Eyes and Ears

Jesus healed the blind. He healed Bartimaeus who had lived as a beggar his entire life. From where he sat, this poor man heard the commotion. People explained it was Jesus coming through the crowd.

He shouted out, "Jesus, Son of David, have mercy on me!"[7] People hushed him, but he shouted all the more.

Jesus noticed him and stopped him. "What do you want me to do for you?" Jesus asked the man.

Bartimaeus said, "I want to see."

Jesus responded, "Go, your faith has healed you."

Immediately, Bartimaeus could see.[8] Jesus healed many other blind people. He healed a man over 40 years old who had been blind since birth, and forced to beg for his daily existence. Jesus spat on the ground and applied mud to his eyes. This time, Jesus performed a two-part healing. At first, the man could only see shapes. After Jesus' second healing touch the man could see clearly.[9]

Jesus opened ears. On one occasion, he healed a deaf and mute man. Jesus stuck his fingers in his ears and he could hear.[10] Jesus also freed a boy from a deaf and mute spirit.[11]

He Healed Lives

Jesus made the lame walk. The most well known story about healing a lame man is that of the paralytic brought by his friends to the house where Jesus was teaching.[12] They ripped a hole in the roof of the house, and lowered the man on his mat to the floor. Jesus saw their faith and told the man his sins were forgiven. The Pharisees and religious leaders took issue with Jesus' words.

Unperturbed Jesus demonstrated his power over the physical, as well as the spiritual. He told the paralyzed man, "Get up, take your mat and go home."[13] Instantly the man was healed. Jesus also healed other lame people, like the man at the Pool of Bethesda.[14] Friends and family brought the lame and crippled and Jesus healed them.[15]

Jesus gave words back to those without a voice. The deaf and mute man did not only receive his hearing, he also was given his voice. Jesus also, in a metaphorical way, gave a voice to women and children—people groups who had no voice in their culture.

He honored women, and he included them with his disciples. Martha's sister, Mary, sat at his feet.[16] She learned like the other disciples. Jesus not only allowed her presence, he encouraged her presence. He prepared all his disciples, including Mary, to be witnesses.

He valued children. Perturbed he rebuked the disciples when they tried to deter children from coming to him, "Let them come to me, and don't hinder them." Then, smiling, Jesus told the children, "Come to me." He blessed them and valued them. In fact, he said to the adults, "Truly I tell you, anyone who will not receive the kingdom of God like a little child will never enter it."[17] These are just a few examples of how Jesus loved, healed, and honored marginalized people.

Jesus freed the possessed. He cast out seven demons from Mary of Magdala.[18] He cast demons out of men, women and children. He set people free from oppression and evil to live fully for God.

Jesus also raised people from the dead. Four days after Lazarus died, Jesus brought him back to life. At another time, Jesus came upon a funeral procession, and he had great compassion for the widow who had lost her only son. He touched the coffin, and he raised the young man from the dead.[19]

Jesus emotionally, physically, mentally and spiritually healed people. These healings were to fulfill the prophecy spoken by Isaiah, when he foretold what the coming of the Messiah would look like:

> Then will the eyes of the blind be opened and the ears of the deaf unstopped. Then will the lame leap like a deer, and the mute tongue shout for joy. Water will gush forth in the wilderness and streams in the desert.[20]

He Ushered in a New Reign

Jesus, the Messiah, came to usher in God's Kingdom. He did not do this on his own. He looked to God for his direction, and he carried out the plans as instructed. Now I don't believe that Jesus, like a modern day quarterback in a football game, received his play calls from the Head Coach moment by moment. We don't know what his communication was with his Father except that he spent time with him. He said that he and his Father were one.[21]

Jesus came to earth to bring redemption and usher in the Kingdom of God. He lived to show what this new Kingdom would look like. He loved people, healed them, taught them, and showed them God's love. He showed them the future Kingdom, and then he needed to die to make it happen. It required him to sacrifice his life—his sinless life. He was sent to live a perfect life and to:

 🐛 demonstrate God's love;

 🐛 teach what it means to love God with all your heart, soul, mind and strength; and

 🐛 love your neighbor as yourself.

He came so that we could live. He had to die to pay the price for all human sin. He had to rise from the dead to bring life and reconciliation.

Was He Really the Messiah?

Jesus was God on earth and here to redeem people. He didn't live the life of a king, but rather he lived the life of a servant. He lived differently than people expected from their promised Messiah. He didn't follow the anticipated script. Even John the Baptist wondered. It's clear that John had been sent to prepare the way for him. He knew God selected him from birth to preach repentance in preparation for the Messiah's coming. He knew the Messiah would arrive in his lifetime. However John, like his fellow Jews that were waiting for the Savior, might have expected a conquering king. John might have also expected he'd live out his days in peace.

When Jesus arrived, John the Baptist knew Jesus was the Lamb of God. He announced it, and he submitted to Jesus' instruction to baptize him. He also knew that it was time for him to become less, and Jesus would take the place of prominence. John expected that to happen, after all, he was sent to *prepare the way* not *be the way*. Yet, as with most everyone called and sent by God, he had expectations of how things would play out. When things turned out differently than expected he wondered... was this the one they were waiting for? Religious leaders opposed Jesus, and John's own life was in danger. He might have questioned himself, "Did I hear and understand God correctly?"

John the Baptist's doubt began after he was imprisoned for speaking out against King Herod's immoral lifestyle. He doubted in spite of having baptized Jesus and testified about him. He had been sure that his task was to prepare the way for the Messiah. He knew at the time of Jesus' baptism that this Jesus was not only his cousin but also "the Lamb of God, who takes away the sin of the world!"[22] John had preached, "Repent for the Kingdom of heaven is near..."[23] People had been prepared for the message of the coming Kingdom by John.[24] Yet, now that John was in prison, he wondered.

Anyone who has followed Jesus in ministry probably has come to a point where questions of doubt started to cause confusion. I've been there.

When life gets tough, and the road does not look anything like I had imagined based on God's call on my life, I've asked, "Did I get it wrong? Did God really call me to do this? Are you sure God? If this is what you have for me to do, why is it so hard? Why is my life falling apart? Why can't I have children? Why do I struggle in my marriage? Why is my child spinning out?"

Once John's vision of what the Messiah would look like didn't happen, John too wondered. When in prison, he started to ask questions. He sent his disciples, those who were still following him and supporting him, to go to Jesus and ask, "Are you the one who was to come, or should we expect someone else?"[25]

Jesus received John's emissaries with kindness, and he gave them what might seem to us a cryptic reply. He said, "Go back and report to John what you hear and see: The blind receive sight, the lame walk, those who have leprosy are cured, the deaf hear, the dead are raised, and the good news is preached to the poor. Blessed is the man who does not fall away on account of me."[26] What did Jesus mean?

John would have understood. After all, he was the one chosen by God prior to birth and given a specific calling, "Prepare the way for the Lord…"[27] John taught the message that the Messiah would come to set his people free. He understood Jesus' message to him in prison as the confirmation that he was the one, the Messiah, that John had proclaimed in the desert. Just like the passage in Isaiah prophesied:

> The Spirit of the Sovereign LORD is on me, because the LORD has anointed me to preach good news to the poor. He has sent me to bind up the brokenhearted, to proclaim freedom for the captives and release from darkness for the prisoners, to proclaim the year of the LORD's favor and the day of vengeance of our God, to comfort all who mourn, and provide for those who grieve in Zion—to bestow on them a crown of beauty instead of ashes, the oil of gladness instead of mourning, and a garment of praise instead of a spirit of despair. They will be called oaks of righteousness, a planting of the LORD for the display of his splendor.[28]

He Is the One!

Jesus came to fulfill God's promises. He was the one—the one John had been waiting for. He lived up to what God intended for him, even if it looked differently than John and the Jewish leaders had expected.

Jesus lived his story to reconcile people to God. He fulfilled prophecy. He preached, "Repent, for the Kingdom of heaven is near."[29] He healed the sick. He set people free. His life showed the Kingdom as "here"—the Kingdom had arrived.

Jesus' coming brought God's Kingdom to earth. He lived his life—his story—publicly. He ushered in a new era, an era of God with us. This era meant people had access to God through Jesus' life while he was on earth. And, after his resurrection, all people had access to God through faith in Jesus.

He came to tangibly demonstrate God's love and live out God's presence among his people. This presented a radical change for the Jews. They had known Jehovah God, the great and awesome God. They knew him to be holy, almighty and powerful. They were his people, but they also feared him. The Old Testament speaks about God's love for his people, but most people experienced this love through his providence and care, not in an intimate relationship. Now Jesus came and lived among them. He touched them, healed them, and loved them. He shared his life with them, and he invited them to share their lives with him.

Jesus loved with a pure love. When his friend, Lazarus, died, he knew that God would raise him. He clearly told his disciples that this sickness would not end in death even though Lazarus experienced death for a short time.

He spoke to both Martha and Mary before he raised Lazarus. First, he talked to Martha and encouraged her. Then he talked to Mary. The book of John tells us, "When Jesus saw her weeping and saw the other people wailing with her, a deep anger welled up within him, and he was deeply troubled."[30] Mary's grief moved Jesus. He didn't prolong the situation. Immediately he asked where they had placed Lazarus' body. They told him to come and see. John records that Jesus wept.[31] He loved Lazarus, Martha and Mary. The love he had for his followers and friends was evident to people around him. When the Jews observed him weeping over Lazarus' situation, they noted, "See how much he loved him!"[32]

One day, when a lawyer asked about the greatest commandment, Jesus told him to, "Love the Lord your God with all your heart and with all your soul and with all your strength and with all your mind," and "Love your neighbor as yourself."[33] Jesus lived the greatest commandment everyday. He loved God with his entire being. He loved his family, friends and followers. He also loved his neighbors—he helped the people God placed on his path. He loved all those whom he came to save.

Toward the end of his life on a day when he approached Jerusalem, he grieved over this city filled with people who were rejecting him. His desire was to gather all of the people like a hen gathers her chicks under her wings.[34] What an illustrative picture of a loving God. There have been cases where a hen was found burned to death with her wings spread wide. When people picked up the dead mother bird, they found live chicks protected under the hen's scorched body. That's the picture Jesus paints of God, the picture of a protective and loving mother bird that gives her life to protect her chicks. Jesus gave his life to save his people—all people. His love extended beyond his friends and followers. He even loved his enemies. On the cross, Jesus said, "Father, forgive them, for they do not know what they are doing."[35]

God the Father sent his son to demonstrate his love to his creation. In the son, God came to earth. Jesus tells his disciples that if they have seen him, they have seen the Father.[36] He lived his story publicly with his followers in response to his Father's leading. He came to reconcile people to God. He showed the visible Kingdom. He allowed people to experience God with us—on earth. He trained his followers to continue to spread the Gospel. Then he completed his assignment and fulfilled his mission of salvation and reconciliation by suffering, dying, and being raised on the third day. That was his mission: to be the perfect Lamb slain for our sin. God "made him who had no sin to be sin for us."[37]

He is the image of the invisible God, the firstborn over all creation. For by him all things were created: things in heaven and on earth, visible and invisible, whether thrones or powers or rulers or authorities; all things were created by him and for him. He is before all things, and in him all things hold together. And he is the head of the body, the church; he is the beginning and the firstborn from among the dead, so that in everything he might have the supremacy. For God was pleased to have all his fullness dwell in him, and through him to reconcile to himself all things, whether things on earth or things in heaven, by making peace through his blood, shed on the cross.[38]

He opened the way to reconciliation for all people by faith in him. He gave this ministry of reconciliation to his disciples. He had lived to demonstrate God's love, bring healing, and call people to repentance. He now sent his disciples to do the same. Before he died, Jesus told his disciples that they would do even greater things than he'd been doing while he was with them on earth.[39] He told them that anything they asked for in his name he would grant them.[40] He told them that he would send another Comforter.[41] He prayed for them. He asked God to protect them by the power of his name, for holiness, and for unity in and through him. Jesus also prayed for all of us who would believe in him.[42]

He Redeemed People's Stories

Jesus touched people's lives and redeemed their brokenness. He transformed their stories. He lived his story amongst them and invested in their lives and stories to accomplish God's best for them. He called people to live their lives on a higher plane. Instead of living according to the Law of Moses, Jesus called people to live a life of love.[43]

Jesus challenged people not only to live by the letter of the law but by the spirit of the law. To be perfect in love[44]—love for God and others. He called them beyond their self-definition to live into all God intended for them.

One afternoon, Jesus invited his disciples to get in the boat with him and go to the other side of the lake. Without warning, a furious squall descended on them. He was unfazed. They were terrified. They imagined the worst. He calmed the storm.[45]

He taught his followers then, and he still teaches us now, that regardless of circumstances, he is capable and controls every aspect of our lives. In the midst of any storm, he is almighty.

The disciples learned that Jesus commanded the wind and the waves. He had told them that they were going to the other side. They didn't expect the intense wind. Jesus probably knew that the storm was coming but, even if he didn't, he knew his Father and his power over all creation. When the squall howled and waves swamped the boat, he remained calm. The disciples panicked. Jesus gently rebuked them, and he asked them, "Where is your faith?" They had just watched his power when he fed a crowd of over 5000 with just five loaves and two fish. Should they have had greater faith by now? Yet, when they saw his power over the wind and the water, they were astonished.

Jesus lived with them, and he demonstrated his care for them, his power over all creation, and his relationship with the Father. He turned them from frightened fishermen to sold-out Jesus-followers.

Jesus called people with unfinished and broken stories to live for him. He invited people to come to him for a higher purpose—redemption and reconciliation to God. He invested in people's lives to bring honor and glory to God. He transformed people's stories. He lived his story to demonstrate God's power and love.

We have unfinished stories. Jesus wants everyone to come to him. He desires to rewrite our unfinished stories for God's glory. Every person who accepts his invitation and trusts in him will be reconciled to God. Every reconciled person's story will be redeemed. Redeemed stories lived publicly bring life and hope to others. Jesus understands every aspect of each person's story. He himself was fully man and faced every temptation. He understood and experienced every feeling, and therefore, he could then and now fully relate to every person. Jesus lived his story perfectly, and he calls us to follow him. He invites us to live our stories for him, with him, and in his Presence.

He called unfinished, unpolished fishermen to become Kingdom ambassadors. He called Peter, a rough, brash fisherman who blundered his way through life. Bold and passionate, Peter stayed close to Jesus. He grew to be one of his closest friends. Yet, he ultimately denied him three times to save his own skin. Jesus called him to a higher level and to a transformed life. He renamed him from Simon to Peter and spoke truth into him. He challenged Peter to love him and take care of his people. Peter responded to Jesus' call, and he fulfilled the role of one of the key leaders in the first church.

He called John. He was a young man, one of two lively brothers. Both were wild-men who relied on aggression to solve problems. Once they asked Jesus if they should call down fire from heaven to destroy a Samaritan town.[46] Jesus had nicknamed him one of the "Sons of Thunder."[47] John was ambitious. He wanted to sit on either Jesus' right or left once he established his Kingdom.[48] He boldly asked for that high position. He wanted to be one of the top guys. Jesus loved this young man. He loved him enough to change him. While following Jesus, John was transformed. Many years later, we see the change in his writings. John refers to himself as the disciple that Jesus loved.[49] He grew in humility, and he focused on living a life of love. His writings call the church to love—love for God and each other. He writes:

> My beloved friends, let us continue to love each other since love comes from God. Everyone who loves is born of God and experiences a relationship with God. The person who refuses to love doesn't know the first thing about God, because God is love—so you can't know him if you don't love. This is how God showed his love for us: God sent his only Son into the world so we might live through him. This is the kind of love we are talking about—not that we once upon a time loved God, but that he loved us and sent his Son as a sacrifice to clear away our sins and the damage they've done to our relationship with God.[50]

Jesus called Matthew who began his career as Levi, the tax collector. He was amongst the hated in Jewish society, yet Jesus called him. He told him to follow. Matthew repented and converted. He brought Jesus his unfinished story, and was transformed into a new man. He ultimately wrote the account of Jesus' life and ministry that we know as the Gospel according to Matthew.

And, Jesus called Paul, a persecutor of Christians who killed or approved of killing many people who followed Jesus. One day, after his resurrection,

Jesus appeared on Paul's (still called Saul) path. He stopped him dead in his tracks, "Saul! Saul! Why are you persecuting me?"

Blinded by the brightest light he'd ever encountered, Paul fell down bewildered, "Who are you, lord?"

The voice he heard from heaven replied, "I am Jesus, the one you are persecuting! Now get up and go into the city, and you will be told what you must do."[51]

Paul was willing to change it all to become the man Jesus wanted him to be. He became the chief evangelist to the Gentile world.

> *Because God is on mission, the people of God are too. God is a sending God. Just as he sent his Son and his Holy Spirit to the world, he is sending his people into the world…The notion of "sentness" lies at the heart of the missional church because it reveals the heart of God.*
>
> —Reggie McNeal

His Story Lives On

Jesus desires to do the same with our lives. He wants to redeem our stories so we, in turn, will tell our stories for the benefit of others. As God sent Jesus into the world, so Jesus has sent us into the world—so people would see and know God's love for them.[52]

While on earth, Jesus taught his disciples to love God and love each other. Jesus sent his disciples to pass on what they had learned. His followers lived their stories to demonstrate the truth of Jesus. They lived out Jesus' love in action and instructed people to obey everything Jesus had taught them. Now he sent them and they, in turn, sent others to continue to spread God's love and bring the ministry of reconciliation. They called others to follow Jesus, as he had called them. This story has continued for over 2,000 years. Jesus-followers are calling people to believe in him and, thereby, new Jesus-followers are recruited into God's service. It's one follower passing it on to others who pass it on. Jesus lived his story to share God's love for his people and reconcile all who believe in him to God. We in turn need to love others with the love of God so they may be reconciled to him.

As John wrote, "My dear, dear friends, if God loved us like this, we certainly ought to love each other. No one has seen God, ever. But if we love one another, God dwells deeply within us, and his love becomes complete in us—perfect love!"[53]

And the story lives on. He calls all who believe in him to live their stories for him so others may come to know him and be reconciled to God.

Living It Out

Jesus is the Messiah who was sent by God. He lived his story as God intended. He came to demonstrate God's love and bring reconciliation. Jesus continues to live his story through his followers, sending them to love as he loved and invite people to be reconciled to God. Henry Blackaby puts it this way, "God is at work reconciling a world to himself. Because he loves you, he wants to involve you in his work. He begins by pursuing a love relationship that is both real and personal. He then invites you to be involved with him."[54]

God loves you and your story. If you know him, are you living your story for him? How are you passing on the story and living to make new followers of Jesus?

Key Concepts

- Jesus came to earth to live his human story publicly and demonstrate God's love.

- His ministry was the ministry of reconciliation—reconciling people to God.

- Jesus invested in people and redeemed the lives and stories of those who believed in him.

- Jesus' story lives in and through his followers.

Questions for Living It Out

1. Have you brought your story to Jesus? Are you living your story for him?

2. How are you living your story to continue his story? How are you passing on his story so that others may become followers of Jesus?

3. Is your story part of Jesus' ministry of reconciliation?

4. Are you actively and intentionally living out Jesus' love for people?

Notes

1. See John 21:25

2. See John 1:1-3

3. Matthew 3:17, NIV

4. See John 5:19, 5:30, 8:28

5. Matthew 4:17, NIV

6. See Isaiah 35:5-6

7. Mark 10:47, NIV

8. See Mark 10:46-52

9. See Mark 8:22-25

10. See Mark 7:31-37

11. See Mark 9:14-27

12. See Luke 5:17-26

13. Luke 5:24, NIV

14. See John 5:1-9

15. See Matthew 15 & 21

16. See Luke 10:38-42

17. Luke 18:17, NIV

18. See Mark 16:9

19. See Luke 7:11-15

20. Isaiah 35: 5-6, NIV

21. See John 17:11

22. John 1:29, NIV

23. Matthew 3:2, NIV

24. See Mark 1:4-8

25. Matthew 11:2-3, NIV

26. Matthew 11:4-6, NIV

27. Mark 1:3, NIV

28. Isaiah 61:1-3, NIV

29. Matthew 4:17, NIV

30. John 11:33, NLT

31. See John 11:35

32. John 11:36, NLT

33. Luke 10:27, NIV

34. See Luke 13:34

35. Luke 23:34, NIV

36. See John 14:9

37. 2 Corinthians 5:21, NIV

38. Colossians 1:15-20, NIV

39. See John 14:12

40. See John 14:14

41. See John 14:16

42. See John 17:6-26

43. See Matthew 5-7

44. See Matthew 5:43-48

45. See Matthew 8:23-37

46. See Luke 9:51-54

47. Mark 3:17, NIV

48. See Mark 10:35-40

49. See John 13:23

50. 1 John 4:7-10, MSG

51. See Acts 9:1-6

52. See John 17

53. 1 John 4:11-12, MSG

54. Henry T. Blackaby and Claude V. King, *Experiencing God: How to Live the Full Adventure of Knowing and Doing the Will of God* (Nashville: Broadman & Holman Publishers, 1994), 39.

Chapter 4

Go Do Some Serious Good

Let us not become weary in doing good, for at the proper time
we will reap a harvest if we do not give up.

—Galatians 6:9, NIV

Jack's Story

Jack, a driven young husband and father, craved success, money, and all the toys that came with an accomplished lifestyle. To reach his goals, Jack spent long days at the office, leaving little time for his family or any other relationships beyond those furthering his career.

His days were organized and started with a perfected morning routine getting him out the door in only twenty minutes, including a quick cup of coffee and breakfast to go. Sales numbers were down, and he needed to close a couple of deals by the end of the week. No time to waste.

Jack quickly kissed his wife, Stacey, looked in on sleeping, Jack Jr., and rushed down the stairs ready to tackle the day. On the third step, he tripped over his son's toy car, tumbled down the stairs, and he landed on the hardwood floor. He distinctly heard a *crack*.

Staring at the ceiling, a sharp pain shot through his right ankle. He sat and then attempted to stand. His ankle screamed in protest, and Jack quickly sat again, taking the pressure off his ankle. He uttered some obscenities then shouted, "Stacey! Come here! Now!"

"Jack, what happened?" Stacey ran down the stairs and knelt by his side.

"I think I broke my ankle," Jack yelped. "Help me up."

Stacey supported him on the side of the broken ankle and hoisted him to his feet. She helped him into their SUV, and then she ran back into the house to grab little Jack Jr., asleep in his bed.

Stacey drove the six miles to the local hospital's emergency room, burying any urge to speed or run a red light.

"Can you go faster?" Jack's voice reflected irritation.

"Not with our precious cargo in the back seat." Stacey stared straight ahead.

"Are you okay, Daddy," Jack Jr.'s lip quivered, as he rubbed sleep out of his eyes.

"Daddy's ankle hurts." *I've got to get a stupid cast put on my ankle, and then I need to get to the office. Of all days…*

"I'm sorry, Daddy."

"Thanks, buddy," Jack offered a thin smile. He thought about hobbling around at work with a cast or brace on his leg and what a total annoyance that was going to be.

They arrived at the hospital. Stacey clasped Jack Jr.'s hand while supporting Jack's full weight and managed to get the three of them into the waiting room and seated. After enduring a long wait, X-rays, several tests, and an active, hungry toddler, the doctor told Jack he needed surgery. He had a bad fracture that required hardware followed by a long-recovery.

"How long a recovery?" Jack squinted, as he attempted to swallow the large lump forming in his throat.

"At least, six weeks." The doctor's voice was flat. "It's a bad break, and it requires intricate surgery to correct. The nurse will get you checked in."

He tucked his pen into the pocket of his white lab coat. He hesitated a moment. "It's important to rest or you'll delay or even permanently damage your recovery." He left the room, closing the door behind him.

Jack turned to face Stacey who mustered an encouraging smile. "We can't afford my taking off work for that long. This is a disaster." He shook his head. "I know you're trying to be brave, but if I can't work, we could lose everything."

"We'll be okay, Jack." Stacey pulled Jack Jr. onto her lap and again smiled. "Don't be borrowing trouble. Let's focus on getting your ankle healed."

Jack sighed. Stacey didn't fully understand the seriousness of their situation. "We could lose everything I've worked for." Jack looked hard into her face. "We're not going to make it."

"Trust, Jack." Stacey clasped his hand and smiled. "We'll be okay."

Jack lay down on the gurney, flopping his head on the pillow. *I can't work and Stacey is in denial. It can't get any worse.* He laced his fingers through his hair. *How can she tell me to trust? Trust what? Does she think money is going to start falling out of the elm tree in our back yard?*

Some people from a local church Jack had never heard of became part of his life for the next six weeks. They brought meals, mowed the lawn, brought groceries, brought his favorite ice cream, and cared for Jack Jr. when Stacey took him for doctor's appointments. Jack sensed a real embarrassment.

He was most surprised and humbled when reconciling the bank statement. "Stacey, did your parents give you some money to help out?" he asked when he noticed unexplained deposits that were enough to cover the bills.

"No, why?" Stacey looked up from putting the dishes away.

"There is extra money in the account. Where did it come from?" Jack's face reflected serious puzzlement. He had not received extra pay from work.

Stacey smiled broadly and said, "Some people from church gave us that money when they found out about our bills. Isn't that something?"

The corners of Jack's mouth turned down. He had always ridiculed people who needed faith and church. He viewed Christians as hypocrites and faith as a crutch. Now, Jack had used this "crutch." The church had provided him with the money he needed for the past six weeks, and he discovered they were the real deal. Church people were caring for and helping him and his family. This reality deeply touched him, and he spent some time alone doing soul-searching about his wrongly held beliefs about church people.

"It's time I reconnect with God and church, as soon as I regain my mobility," Jack confessed to Stacey. "I'll join you and my little man on Sundays."

Stacey beamed. "Going to church as a family is an answer to prayer." The church had welcomed her and little Jack with open arms.

Valley View Church had reached out to help them. They heard about Jack's accident through an email from one of Jack and Stacey's neighbors. People of the church were active in their neighborhood, and they had fully responded to reach out to a "not-yet friend" of Jesus.

Several of their people signed up for the various tasks and loved the idea of serving Jack and showing him the real Jesus. They believed in doing "serious good." Their motto was, "Looks like sacrifice, feels like love."[1] They chose to love Jack and his family because Jesus loved them. They were trained, ready to volunteer, and dedicated to being a loving community to Jack. Valley View people were intentional about showing Jesus' love, and they committed for the duration.

"Stacey, some guys from the church just called," Jack mentioned. He was feeling much better. "They're having a men's event. What do you think? Should I go?"

"Absolutely. They've been great to us."

"They said they'd pick me up," Jack responded sheepishly. Driving was still a little difficult. He couldn't wait to be fully healed, but he appreciated everything the people from church had done for him. He was ready to re-connect and maybe become part of the community that loved and helped him and his family during his time of need.

What Is "Serious Good"?

Most people want to help their neighbor or do something good in their community. There are many people giving their lives to really making a difference by helping the homeless, loving their neighbors, working in food banks, tutoring children, and more. Many of us look up to people who give their lives to these endeavors, but we don't necessarily have the passion, drive or time to invest in the same way. When I see others seriously volunteering, I feel guilty—but not guilty enough to step up to the same extent.... Yet I believe in doing serious good.

Serious good requires intentionality and commitment. It is the kind of good the people from Valley View Church showed to Jack when he broke his ankle. It's the kind of good God talks about in Micah 6:8, "He has showed you, O man, what is good. And what does the LORD require of you? To act justly and to love mercy and to walk humbly with your God."

Serious good involves love in action. It means being just. It means loving mercy. It means looking to God for our cues on how to love our neighbors.

Jesus had in mind that the *serious good* we should do is demonstrating God's love in such a way that people would see his love in action and be drawn to him. Jesus tells us we should live a life of love[2] to draw people to God and live as witnesses.

> This is what it's going to take to gain a hearing for the gospel in the streets of the twenty-first century—the smell of cleaning solution, dirty faces, obvious acts of servant hood.
>
> —Reggie McNeal

Go. Do. Some. Serious. Good.

To Valley View Church, *doing serious good* enabled them to live out Jesus' commandments and to actively demonstrate God's love.

Jesus sends us to: *Go Do Some Serious Good.*

Go

The Great Commission tells us to, "Go and make disciples"[3] or more precisely, "While going, make disciples."[4] The method of our going should be in line with everything else Jesus commanded. He sends and instructs us to go as we love God and each other. When we go this way, people can see and experience Jesus. We need to "go" the way Jesus demonstrated and the disciples lived—as recorded in the book of Acts.

Jesus tells us to make our lives count. The Great Commission sends us to live intentionally—so that "while we are going" we live a life of meaning. We need to live a life of love especially with fellow Christians. Why? Jesus tells us to love one another. When we live in such a way that we exude Jesus' love, it will draw people to Jesus through us. This means we have to live this love out publicly and authentically. When people see the love we have for each other, it will attract them. But loving each other is not enough.

Jesus commands us to love each other and he commands us to "go." The call is to go and reach people for Jesus in every community. How can we do that? One easy way is through acts of service to our neighbors and our community. Most people do not want us to come and knock on their doors and tell them about God, Jesus or the Bible. (Of course, most of us don't want to go and knock on people's doors either.) However, most people are receptive to loving acts of service. And, in general, people do not resist prayers offered on their behalf to ease their life struggles.

A great way to "go" is to serve people in our sphere of influence. That might be our neighborhood, community, friends and family. Studies show that a majority of people would not mind hearing about Jesus from their friends and family. Imagine that! This presents a great open door. Now, if we love and live a life of service to our loved ones, this might provide the evidence and platform to have the discussions and tell them about the real Jesus who transforms lives. Loving actively through serving creates this platform.

Do

But what should we actually *do*? Let's do whatever God leads us to do. The specific tasks depend on the situation and the people involved.

What's most important is that we serve out of love for Jesus and not for self-oriented reasons. Genuine service is in response to Jesus' Great Commission. It's about our love for him. Only then will we be able to make disciples and teach them to fully obey Jesus.

Ultimately, God invites us to do anything that is good to do while we are "going." We are God's artwork, which he created. Just as he determined our shape before the creation of the world, he also decided what it is we should be doing in his world and for his Kingdom. As Paul taught, "For we are God's workmanship, created in Christ Jesus to do good works, which God prepared in advance for us to do."[5] God knows the good he has for each one of us to do. He knows what is required to accomplish his ultimate plan. We can join him if we are willing, and he has specific things for us to contribute. Our contributions should be discovered in our relationship with him and flow out of that relationship. As the Psalmist tells us, "Trust in the LORD and do good."[6] Our significance comes from God and our identity with him. As we spend time with him, it will become exceedingly clear what it is he wants us to do.

We're designed and wired by God in unique ways. He has not only prepared the works, he also prepared us specifically for those works. (More in Chapter 6, *Grow into Your Original Design.*) Therefore, since we have been created to do good works God prepared for us, our significance should not come from the work nor the people we do good for or with. Doing good means we love and serve in response to God, out of our love for him, without looking to receive significance or reward from people as we serve them. Our service should flow out of our relationship with God, with our significance coming from God, and from our identity in him.

A friend and fellow pastor, Josh Hebert, spoke about how Jesus modeled this after receiving God's blessings following his baptism as recorded in Matthew 3.

> As soon as Jesus was baptized, he went up out of the water. At that moment heaven was opened, and he saw the Spirit of God descending like a dove and lighting on him. And a voice from heaven said, 'This is my Son, whom I love; with him I am well pleased.'[7]

Based on this account, Josh mentioned, "From this moment on Jesus wasn't living seeking approval but was living from approval." As Jesus' followers, we too should live our Christian lives based on the sure knowledge that we are children of God, and as such, loved and approved by him. Therefore, our good works should flow out of our love and relationship with him. He loves us and is pleased with us. We do our good works not to make or keep God happy but rather to bring him glory and demonstrate his love to our neighbors, friends and family.

"For in Christ Jesus neither circumcision nor uncircumcision has any value. The only thing that counts is faith expressing itself through love."[8] This verse uses the Greek word, *agape*, for love. This kind of love is unconditional and expresses itself in action. It is not a feeling.

Doing good is not limited. God wants us to do good to all people—believers and unbelievers. Now most of us do not struggle (as much) with doing good to our fellow Christians. Most church communities have ways and systems to take care of their own. Through benevolence, a church word for financial assistance, people in the church who are falling on hard times can often receive some help. Through small groups, people are cared for in a smaller community, which includes support, prayer, encouragement, relational, and even physical or tangible help. The Bible is clear. We are sent to do good to fellow believers:

> Let us not become weary in doing good, for at the proper time we will reap a harvest if we do not give up. Therefore, as we have opportunity, let us do good to all people, especially to those who belong to the family of believers.[9]

But, it cannot stop there. For so many of us in the church, doing good is limited to our friends and church family. While this is important it cannot be the entire picture. How will people know of God's love if we don't share it? We need to go beyond our own. We are not to grow weary in doing good. Jesus commands us to love God and love our neighbor. Our neighbor is more than another church member. Who is our neighbor? It is anyone who God puts on our path.

For several years, I served as pastor of adult ministries at a local church. My responsibilities included small groups, as well as care and assistance.

Our groups were structured as life groups with covenants but also as side doors to the church. The goal for every small group was to be a welcoming place for people who were not yet part of our church community. The groups understood this component and a percentage had people in the group who were still finding their way back to God. However, there wasn't much success in bringing people into a saving relationship with Jesus.

As God stretched my understanding of his heart for the community around us, he gave me a bigger vision. As a result, we started to expand our care and assistance to reach outside the church walls. We intentionally structured it to include people beyond church attenders. God allowed us to come alongside people in real life situations. We loved them practically and demonstrated God's love through compassion, care and prayer. Through extending love to our neighbors, God brought several people into a saving relationship with Jesus. As we saw this work, my passion for reaching people who are "not-yet friends" of Jesus through service grew.

> *In a typical week, only one out of every four believers will allocate some time to serving other people. Most of that time is dedicated to volunteering in church programs that serve congregants; little effort is invested in serving needy people outside the congregation.*
>
> *— George Barna*

During this time, I enrolled at Fuller Theological Seminary in their Master of Arts in Global Leadership (MAGL) degree program. God clearly led me this way. My passion was leadership, and I had hoped to earn a leadership degree with a missional focus. It turned out to be a missional degree with a leadership focus. It was just what I needed.

Using my studies, God warmed my heart toward missional ministry. In fact, he reminded me of who I had been all along. As I learned about going into the community and living a transparent life in the midst of people, it started to remind me of something. In fact, more and more this idea and concept seemed strangely familiar. During one class, it dawned on me that I grew up in a postmodern, post-Christian society and had lived a missional life when I was a child. I grew up in the Netherlands—a place where kids (and grown-ups) didn't talk about God and not many people in my environment went to church. At that time, church attendance was probably around 25-40 percent.[10] For some reason, I did talk about God all the time. He was totally real to me. In this context, talking to people about faith wasn't about trying to get them to pray a prayer or sharing the four spiritual laws. God just was part of my life, and I shared who he was and how I experienced him. I talked about him as I would a friend because he was real to me.

While going through the MAGL program, I "learned" that in order to engage the increasingly post-Christian and postmodern society in the U.S., we needed to change our approach. We needed to live our faith and demonstrate God's love through our life stories. My big question to myself was, "How did I get lost? I knew this before. What happened?"

I think in some ways the church happened. I immigrated to a modern, Christian society. So, I adapted to my new culture and accepted this way of "doing church" as the right way. Unfortunately, I lost my missional mindset, approach, and lifestyle. There were minor remnants, but these were just shadows of what had been. Then in the MAGL program, I was reminded about living missionally. Toward the end, as I re-embraced living missionally and demonstrating God's love to the world through practical involvement (in other words through doing good), God showed me a new picture.

In one of my final classes, during an exercise to come up with a vision for our various ministries, I was thinking about what my vision would be. Suddenly, this statement was placed into my thoughts: "A missional army of empowered leaders, impassioned for God, unleashed into enemy territory to impact every community for Christ through the power of the Holy Spirit."

That's it! That is what it is all about. My mission was an army of leaders serious about God and living it out in community. It's about spiritually mature, serious leaders living their stories in such a way that people catch the vision and passion to spread God's love to every community. Leaders leading people to live their stories so people everywhere are exposed to eternal life in a way that makes them interested and curious.

It requires people living it out together. Living missionally intentionally. Doing good on purpose. Letting people experience Jesus through acts of service. Not just one person at a time, but as a collective group, a collaborative community…the body of Christ.

Jesus sent us to be the Church. God poured out his Spirit on Jesus, and he has given us the same Spirit. God approved of Jesus, and he approves of us. And, if God is for us, who can be against us?[11] We have all we need to go and do as God leads us.

God sends us and equips us fully:
- Jesus through us,
- God for us,
- The Spirit in us.

The Apostle Paul clearly tells us God has justified us.[12] We have peace with God through Jesus. We are saved from God's wrath through Jesus. We have access to God through faith in Jesus. We are standing in God's grace through Jesus. God has poured out his love into our hearts by the Holy Spirit. God has given us what we need to do—what he intends for us to do.

Some

We don't have to do all the good by ourselves. When I taught about spiritual gifts, I would tell people that no one gets all the gifts. This is good news because if we had all of them, we might be expected to do everything! God didn't design life that way. He made us a body of believers—the Church. Each of us is an aspect, a part, of that body.

We don't have to do everything in the body. We only need to do *our* part in the body. We need to do what our particular part is designed to do. If we are eyes, we are assigned to see. If we are ears, it is our job to listen and be there for people. If we are hands, we need to serve and help. If we are feet, we should go for a walk and do something. If we are…well, you get the picture.

We can take great comfort from Ephesians 2:10, which tells us, we are God's art project made by him for the purpose *he* created us for. God decided when he made each of us, the exact jobs and tasks he wanted us to do. To each he assigned what he or she is capable of doing. As the parable of the servants demonstrated, the owner of the house gave each one according to his ability. He also expected each of them to live up to that ability!

Of course, we all know we have to live within limits. There are limits to our physical, mental, and emotional energies. As part of being called, we need to live wisely, trusting God to give us enough but not too much. Limits are important.

The point is we are all sent to do SOME good. Our part. And when we each do our part, all of it will be done. At last count there are over seven billion people in the world. According to some, there are about one billion Christians in the world. Furthermore, we all are six people removed from everyone else in the world (six degrees of separation). That made me think—if each Christian has an impact on six or seven non-Christians we could reach all people. Think about that! No one can reach all seven billion people for Christ. We all just need to reach *some*.

This helps me because sometimes I become overwhelmed by all the needs in the world. Seeing all the pain and suffering causes me to want to make it all go away, but there is no way I can even hope to make a dent. None of us can. However, if we all do our part and give our portion, we can influence and reduce (or even remove) the needs in every community. If all American Christians tithed,[13] giving God back 10% of his money, the Church would have billions of dollars to alleviate hunger, solve water issues, and much more.

According to Richard Stearns, president of World Vision U.S., there would be an extra $168 billion[14] available for serious good around the world. He gives compelling statistics of what this money could accomplish: $65 billion "could eliminate the most extreme poverty on the planet for more than a billion people"; $9 billion could bring clean water to most of the world's poor; $13 billion could provide basic health and nutrition for everyone.[15] Just think, after doing those three there still would be $81 billion left over!

These numbers clearly show if all of us did SOME good things—give some (10%), love some (affect seven people who don't know God), and do some (contribute our gifts and skills in some worthwhile fashion)—

people in the world would be transformed and physically experience the love of Jesus. Now that's something I can get excited about!

> *Jesus believes the kingdom of God is present. This can mean only one thing: he expects his followers to live in the kingdom in their daily lives—right now. Thus, a spiritually formed follower of Jesus lives the values of the kingdom now.*
>
> —Scot McKnight

Serious

No one wants to waste his time or his life. I know for me, if it's not going to make a difference or have an impact then why bother? Of course this could be perceived as arrogance and elitism since there definitely is a role for the mundane, routine, and even tedious in our lives. Not everything we are part of or participate in can be glorious and high impact. Most of life is lived in the dailies—putting our feet on the road or the hand on the wheel and just going. It's not about the avoidance of repetitive tasks or even simple, insignificant tasks. It is when all the tasks, whether grand or simple, do not add up to anything of value.

If I am going to spend my time and energy on something I want it to count. This is especially true when it comes to God's Kingdom. Why go through the motions? Why just "play" at the Christian life? Jesus died for us to have life…shouldn't we give our lives to something worthwhile in return? If we were worth dying for, shouldn't our lives be worth living— really living? When I have to answer the question of how I spent my time during the dash between my birth date and my earthly expiration date, I would like to have a solid answer for the King of Kings. One day, we'll have to give an account for how we lived down here. He already knows how we spent our "dash" time, but we will still have to account not only for every action but also every word. Jesus told the Pharisees, "But I tell you that men will have to give account on the day of judgment for every careless word they have spoken."[16] The Apostle Paul writes, "So then, each of us will give an account of himself to God."[17]

The idea of giving an accounting of all my days at the end of my life has always affected me. The day I stand before Jesus, I want to be able to bring him the gift of a life well lived. When I read the parable of the servants, I want to be the good and faithful servant. In the end I want to hear, "Well done!" So what does it mean to live such a life? How is living the life of Jesus' faithful servant accomplished?

It's clear salvation isn't accomplished through acts of service or good behavior. We know and believe it is through grace we have been saved by faith, not by works so no one can boast about it.[18] So living a good life is not to obtain salvation, but rather as a result of salvation. Living a worthwhile life should flow out of our relationship with Jesus. It's because he has given us life and called us to follow him. He has asked us to be disciples—loving like him, making new disciples, and teaching them all about Jesus and following him.

The Apostle Paul tells us to live lives worthy of the calling we have received.[19] What is "worthy of the calling"? What does a life like that look like? According to Paul, we are to love like Christ loved and live a life of love.[20] Jesus told us to love God and love our neighbor. In fact, we are to love our neighbor as ourselves. Love is not an emotion but requires action. It means doing *good* to the family of God and to those who do not yet belong to the household of faith.

In the Western world, we often think of love as an emotion. It signifies how we feel about a person or situation. If we love something, we want to do it. If we love someone, we want to be with him or her. But this is not the love Jesus talks about in John 13: 34 and 35. He demonstrated a different kind of love. The love Jesus exemplified meant sacrifice to the point of death. His disciples understood Jesus' example and his teachings.

Jesus said to follow him meant to pick up our cross daily and dying to self. The disciples were willing to be jailed, persecuted, and die for their faith. Paul gives us a litany of experiences that include being flogged, jailed, ridiculed, stoned, ship wrecked, and more. In the end, he died for his faith. Peter reputedly was crucified upside down.

I'm not saying we'll have to pay the ultimate sacrifice for the sake of Jesus, as we live as Christ-followers though some will. What I'm saying is Jesus talks about an active love that benefits the recipient.

Paul commends the church at Colosse because of their faith and how they lived it out. In fact, he thanked God for them and kept praying for them:

> So ever since we first heard about you we have kept on praying and asking God to help you understand what he wants you to do; asking him to make you wise about spiritual things; and asking that the way you live will always please the Lord and honor him, so that you will always be doing good, kind things for others, while all the time you are learning to know God better and better.[21]

Doing serious good is all about pleasing the Lord and bringing honor and glory to him. This will result in us striving to always do good and kind things for others. In the process, we'll get to know God better and better. And others will experience God's love through us.

Doing serious good includes loving and caring for our family and friends. Paul admonishes Timothy to teach the church under his leadership to care for the widows in their midst. The church needed to care for their own widows—as well as those in the community I assume—who had no one else. However, he also makes it clear that if "a widow has children or grandchildren, these should learn first of all to put their religion into practice by caring for their own family and so repaying their parents and grandparents, for this is pleasing to God."[22] Imagine a community like that in our world where kids and grandkids took care of their elderly parents. What a testimony to the community around them!

I know of several families that have their parents living with them, and they're caring for them. It stands out because it is unusual. That is a sad statement about the way believers are living these days. In the first century, families probably had similar issues and challenges. Parents failed their kids. Kids disappointed their parents. Yet, Paul didn't put in a caveat that allows us to wiggle off the hook if our parents were less than ideal during our growing up years. James, the brother of Jesus, described this as true religion—looking after orphans and widows in their distress and not being polluted by the world.[23]

For each person and family how we respond in faith to care for our relatives and close friends probably plays out differently. However, it is obvious God intends us to do good to our family, friends, the church, and people in our surroundings.

Doing serious good means living missionally intentionally amongst our neighbors. This might mean bringing meals, helping kids with homework, sharing life, helping with errands, inviting people over for dinner, helping with the yard, etc. It means leading efforts to make our neighborhoods safer. It means sharing God's love, comfort, peace, and joy. It means inconveniencing ourselves on behalf of those who do not yet know him—so they may see him, experience him and, hopefully one day, reconnect with him.

Good

How can we do some serious good? Many of us know God tells us to care for the widow, orphan, and the poor. Jesus tells us to love our neighbors as we love ourselves. Doing good work requires us to live our faith in practical ways.

We all live in a community or neighborhood. We have certain friends. We were born into a family. We connect with people through our work or profession. And we have contact with people as we shop, get gas, or dine in a restaurant. We encounter people in our every day lives. This "community" of people around us has needs and those needs present opportunities for doing good.

It makes sense to have an impact on the people in our sphere—that is probably why we have a sphere. Sometimes we think doing good and being missional requires going to another country or benefiting people in remote locations. Of course, helping the poorest of the poor in India, Africa, and other places is worthwhile and necessary. But in a way, isn't it also easier? Isn't it less of a personal cost or an investment of ourselves to live missionally for a week during a mission trip or when we send money to a worthy cause than it is to live missionally every day of the year with people that know us?

During a workshop I attended, God convicted me several times that my son had been right about doing good and being generous, and I was the one getting it wrong. He'd been working full days and giving his money to a homeless couple because they were destitute. I had been worried about him not saving and paying us back on debts he owed us. We could use the money, but they needed it. So, when I got home I talked to him. I told him of the conviction and said, "You've been getting it right, and I've been getting it wrong. It must have been confusing to have the Christian grown-ups being against helping these poor people."

My son shrugged his shoulders at my question, and he said, "Yeah. It kind of does, Mom."

Sometimes I fall in the trap of thinking what I'm doing is wonderful and people should appreciate my good deeds. I did help this poor couple, and I thought my help was enough. I thought: *They don't know how good they have it.* My prideful attitude about the good works possessed an undertone of "I'm owed gratitude." My generosity may sometimes start in the right place, but ends up in an ugly place.

If we do good works, give to the poor—or if we can employ down and out people in our homes or workplace—whatever it is we do, we need to do it for the right reason without trying to be seen as wonderful people. If we do our acts of kindness to get rewarded, then we're taking the glory, instead of giving God all the glory. Our deeds and love will be their own witness.

If I want to serve, it's only right I perform that service for the right reasons without talking about it or acting like it's amazing. This is especially true when our service is truly amazing.

> *Dear Lord, Thank you for this insight. I'm sorry I have taken the glory that belongs to you and made it all about me. Please forgive me. Thank you for the privilege of walking alongside the people you've place in my life. Thank you for the blessings you've bestowed on our lives. Help us to be good stewards. In Jesus' Name, Amen.*

Doing serious good is our daily commitment when we believe in Jesus. If we choose to intentionally do good as the Lord leads, we have the opportunity to positively impact people's lives through our acts of service. We have an opportunity to demonstrate Jesus' love to others. It's a chance to live out our gratitude and demonstrate the difference Jesus makes in our lives every single day.

Many of us know the parable of the Good Samaritan.[24] To the Jewish hearers this was an offensive story. Samaritans were half-breeds they despised. Now Jesus, the great rabbi, tells the story of a Good Samaritan who is better than the Jewish clergy and church leaders. Scandalous!

The people who should've taken care of the dying man on the road out of Jerusalem stayed far away from him. They deliberately avoided him. Stopping to help him didn't fit in their lives or daily schedule. They didn't want to mess up their clothes and get "unclean" because it would hinder their ability to serve God. They left the guy to die.

Who were these men? One was a priest and the other a lay leader in the "church." Neither one stopped to care for the down and out, the guy in their "neighborhood" that had been beaten by robbers. Then the unlikely hero arrived; the one who was seen as an unbeliever and outcast—a person who was not part of "our church." He chose to stop and inconvenience himself to help the man who was left to die. He messed up his plans, spent his own money, and cared for the man. He was a neighbor to the man who needed help.

That is our call and responsibility. Faith should demonstrate itself in good deeds. In fact, if we don't live out our faith in good deeds, God considers that sin—plain and simple. Jesus' brother, James, writes, "Anyone, then, who knows the good he ought to do and doesn't do it, sins."[25] That is a clear statement! So what do we do? Each one of us can start right where we are.

How does our story fit in our community? The question we need to ask is, "Who can I be a neighbor to?" It's more than looking at who happens to live next door to me. Let's ask, "Who does Jesus want us to share his love with? Who should we serve? Who should we do some serious good for so that person may experience the love of Jesus?"

It requires looking around. Who is around us in our lives? Who do we interact with on a daily or regular basis? What are their needs? What are our interests and skills? (For more on the concept of doing good according to your wiring, see Chapter 6, *Grow into Your Original Design*.)

Let's live like the Valley View Church folks did with Jack in our story when they met him based on his needs. They gave money, brought groceries, provided childcare, listened, supported Stacey, mowed the lawn, etc. The most sustainable way to do good and volunteer is when you do it as part of your life and according to the way you are wired. It's about the Great Commission, "As you go" or "while going…"

love people, help people, and affect people with the love of Jesus.

Living It Out

Do you know your community? If not, maybe that could be your first step. Look around. Who has God placed on your path? Get to know them and their story. Find out how you can connect with them, and what they need based on who you are and what you're able to do. If you know your community, that's a good start! Are you connected with them? How can you practically do serious good and demonstrate Jesus' love as part of your normal life? If you are a leader, how can you use your gifts and skills to lead others to join you in doing some serious good?

Our stories need to be lived in the midst of our community so people can experience the truth and reality of Jesus. God longs for his children to be reconciled to him. He chose us to be the instruments of his reconciliation. We're called by Jesus to go and do some serious good. We're called to touch people. We're called to actively share the love of Christ.

One real way to allow people to experience the life-changing love of Christ is through the practical love of his people. We're sent so people in our sphere can experience Jesus through our acts of service. We're not to do this alone. We're called to live as a body and do acts of service together. Our stories need to be lived out loud. Let's not stay stuck, silent, and living in boxes. God blesses and helps those who live out their faith through doing serious good. It's a life worth living when we're doing practical acts of service for those around us in Jesus' name.

Key Concepts

વ્§ God made us and prepared good things for us to do.

વ્§ Jesus tells us to go and share his life and love with others.

વ્§ One great way to love others is by doing serious good—living missionally intentionally.

વ્§ All of us have a part, and we only have to do our part.

વ્§ Let's do serious good in response to God and for his glory.

Questions for Living It Out

1. Do you have a Jack and Stacey in your life? Who can you be a good neighbor to? Who are you drawn to?

2. Have you done an inventory of your sphere of influence and discovered which people God has placed in your life?

3. Do you know your community?

4. Who could you do some serious good for or with so they can experience Jesus' love in action? Are you intentionally connecting with people or opportunities that fit your passion so you can live out Jesus' love in service?

5. How can you practically do serious good and demonstrate Jesus' love as part of your normal life?

Notes

1. Pastor Josh Hebert, Lead Pastor, Life at the Ridge, Redmond, WA, 2010.

2. See John 13:34-35

3. Matthew 28:19, NIV

4. Freeman, Robert. 2005. *ML582: Global Leadership in Context.* MAGL. Fuller Theological Seminary, Pasadena, CA.

5. Ephesians 2:10, NIV

6. Psalm 37:3, NIV

7. Matthew 3:16-17, NIV

8. Galatians 5:6, NIV

9. Galatians 6:9-10, NIV

10. Knippenberg, Hans, and Sjoerd de Vos. March 27, 2008 (first published online). *Spatial Structural Effects on Dutch Church Attendance.* Wiley Online Library. John Wiley & Sons, Inc. http://onlinelibrary.wiley.com/doi/10.1111/j.1467-9663.1989.tb01733.x/ abstract. *Tijdschrift voor Economische en Sociale Geografie.* June 1989. Vol. 80. Issue 3, page 164. Accessed online Aug. 30, 2011.

11. See Romans 8:31

12. See Romans 5:1-9

13. Currently about 4 percent of Christians tithe. Source: The Barna Group, *Donors Proceed with Caution, Tithing Declines.* May 10, 2011. http://www.barna.org/donorscause-articles/486-donors-proceed-with-caution-tithing-declines?q=study+shows+trends+ti thing+donating. Accessed online Sep. 29, 2011.

14. Richard Stearns, *The Hole in Our Gospel* (Nashville: Thomas Nelson, 2009), 218.

15. ibid.

16. Matthew 12:36, NIV

17. Romans 14:12, NIV

18. See Ephesians 2:8-9

19. See Ephesians 4:1

20. See Ephesians 5:1

21. Colossians 1:9-10, TLB

22. 1 Timothy 5:4, NIV

23. See James 1:27

24. See Luke 10:30-37

25. James 4:17, NIV

Chapter 5

Demonstrate His Love in Community

A joy shared is a joy doubled.

—Goethe

And let us not neglect our meeting together, as some people do, but encourage one another, especially now that the day of his return is drawing near.

—Hebrews 10:25, NLT

Maria's Story

When it came to living her life well, Maria valued family and hard work. She embraced the attributes of what it takes to live as a good person. When she was a child, she had been confirmed into the Catholic church. Her mom had encouraged her to attend church and be a good Catholic, and it made sense to Maria.

She loved her husband, Jay, spent time with friends, and professionaly did well in the work place. Life was generally good, but something seemed to be missing. She believed the void came from not having children. She and her husband struggled with infertility. Unfulfillment bubbled under the surface.

One day, her friend, Ellie, invited her to church. Maria wasn't sure she should attend a church that met in a school.

She smiled a small smile, and asked Ellie, "Is it a Catholic church?"

"No. It's great though," Ellie said with a smile stretched across her face. She moved a little closer to Maria and said, "You and Jay will love it, believe me." She touched Maria's arm and locked her gaze.

"I'll ask Jay," Maria said, averting her eyes. "But, please know that my husband isn't much of a church-goer."

To her surprise Jay said he'd go, and that clinched the deal for her. She wanted to attend church as a couple. This church was a start-up, and the pastor preached practical, down-to-earth sermons immediately applicable to their lives. She liked being at this church more than she had ever liked church before. Overall, Maria enjoyed her life, and she believed adding going to church would please God and make things better.

To her surprise and confusion, her personal life started to derail. She and Jay continued to deal with infertility. On top of this ordeal, her mom was diagnosed with cancer and the outlook was bleak. Anger and sadness consumed her.

"Ellie, why are these bad things happening to Jay and me?" Maria's voice quivered, fighting to keep the tears welling up in her eyes from traveling down her cheeks. "We're trying really hard to be good people. Bad things aren't supposed to happen to good people, right?"

Ellie hugged Maria, and she whispered gently in her ear, "Just trust God."

Maria tried to trust God, but over the next few years the difficulties increased. Her mom continued to lose her battle with cancer. Maria conceived several times, but all her pregnancies ended in miscarriages. Grief was a constant companion. Shortly after the fourth miscarriage, her mom died of cancer. Life lost all of its joy. She struggled with her faith, but she dutifully continued attending church.

One Sunday, the pastor encouraged everyone to sign up for a group. Ellie cornered her after the service, "Maria, you should sign up for a group. I'll go with you!"

Maria hesitated, unsure if she could handle anything this intimate when she was going through such misery. "I guess I could."

Ellie pulled her over to the small group table, and with enthusiasm, she said, "Let's join a women's group."

Maria nodded, and she signed her name on the sheet. Secretly, she hoped she would never hear from anyone. But later in the week, she received a call from one of the small group leaders. She agreed to attend the group with Ellie the following week, but she had serious reservations.

Over the next few years, Maria faithfully attended and participated in the group, becoming friends with the women. She also took the Bible study seriously, and she learned to apply the Word of God to her life. She asked many questions about heaven, death, suffering, God, Jesus, and the Holy Spirit. She learned to believe that Jesus is God, that heaven is a real place, and the Holy Spirit is the third Person of the Trinity who is active in her life. She loved this group, which allowed her to ask the tough questions without judging her or making her feel stupid. But she would soon wonder if she could truly trust them.

Maria became pregnant again and the group celebrated. Several weeks later, Maria found out that the baby had severe birth defects and would have no quality of life. She withdrew from the group and church. She and Jay tried to pray and do the right thing. They were confused and scared. The hospital staff encouraged them to end the pregnancy and, after much agonizing over the choices they faced, they did.

Maria "knew" the group would judge her so she stayed away even though Ellie tried to convince her to come back. Maria refused. She knew the women in the group had been against the decision and had encouraged her to trust God with the pregnancy. She and Jay had not chosen that route, and now she did not want to hear their condemnation or see their disapproval. She isolated from her Christian family determined to go it alone.

However, the group members lovingly persisted to reach out to her. They called her and encouraged her to come back. One day, she and Ellie attended a birthday celebration with members of her small group. Instead of disapproval, she experienced love, acceptance and comfort. Instead of judgment, she received compassion and care. The group's response floored Maria and deeply affected her.

That abortion changed the trajectory of her future. She turned fully to Jesus and grew in her knowledge and relationship with him. Soon she volunteered on the children's ministry team. After a few years, she joined the church staff as director of care and assistance. Jay was very proud of her. He had continued to grow too and fully supported her. Maria found her niche. Her passion was to help women going through tough times and come alongside families who were dealing with cancer.

One day, she met Sandy, a neighbor whose daughter Megan had been diagnosed with recurring ovarian cancer while pregnant with her second child. Maria prayed with Sandy and offered to visit Megan. Over the next few months, Maria cared for Megan and her family. She arranged for meals and provided help. She also partnered with people in the church and local nonprofits to provide the assistance the family needed. Megan had her baby safely, but she couldn't beat her cancer. Things were going down hill fast.

Maria kept caring for Megan and her family. After a while, the entire family started coming to church. Megan was pleased that her husband Mark finally wanted to join her at church. The joy was brief.

Too soon for everyone involved Megan ended up in the hospital. She was ready for the final stages, but she wanted to take care of some important issues before her imminent death. When Maria visited her, she beckoned her to come close and sit on the bed. "After I accepted Jesus, I never was baptized," she said softly, her voice failed her as she tried to keep from crying. "And the baby has not been dedicated yet. Is there a way we can still do that? You're a pastor right?" Her countenance filled with anguish.

Maria leaned closer and gently touched Megan's hand. "We can do it here in this room! I would be honored to baptize you and dedicate your baby," she said, choking up but smiling. She lightly squeezed Megan's hand, seeing the relief in the dying woman's eyes.

She organized the event and performed both ceremonies in the hospital room. She also served Megan communion. It was a first for both of them— Megan's first time to take communion and Maria's first time to serve it.

Megan's last deep concern was that Mark didn't really believe, and he hadn't accepted Jesus. Megan hung on while Mark adjusted to the inevitable. On her daily visits, he kept asking Maria questions about God. In the process of Megan's cancer, Mark learned to trust Jesus.

One day, Maria took the plunge realizing Megan's time was very short, she told Mark boldy, "You have watched Megan's joy even with the cancer. You know she loves Jesus." She paused, looking directly at Mark and waited for an answer.

He looked at her and nodded. "Yes, I have," he said, his voice confident.

"Are you ready to invite Jesus into your life? You know it's one of Megan's dying wishes." Maria placed her hand on Mark's shoulder.

Mark swallowed, averted her gaze, and said in a low voice, "Yes, I am."

Maria took his hand and suggested, "Why don't we pray together and make it official?" Mark nodded, and they prayed.

Megan had been listening to Mark repeating the words. A smile spread over her face, as tears ran down her cheeks. She motioned to Mark. He came over and gently hugged his crying wife.

Megan did not live long after this special time. The family grieved over the loss, and Maria continued to be there for them. The family eagerly embraced her love and support from the church. A few months after Megan's death, Mark was baptized during a church service.

Maria shared her life and demonstrated Jesus' love to Megan's family. She and Jay had experienced mercy and grace. God used her painful experiences to make a difference in other people's lives, and he brought her healing too. She didn't force conversations about Jesus—she simply loved the people God put on her path. In loving them came the opportunities to share Jesus. She tried to be ready to give an answer to anyone who asked about her life and her love for Jesus.[1] She strove to live in such a way that people would ask questions. Maria told people about the love of Jesus through her actions and with her words.

Tell Your Story in Community

Maria's story is lived out by people who love Jesus and embrace a desire to make a Kingdom difference. Our stories when lived out with others, tell the truth about God's goodness, his love for people, and the Good News of Jesus.

Consider the following questions:

- ✎ What stories are we telling?

- ✎ Are we giving our stories and our challenges to Jesus so he can demonstrate his love and grace to and through us?

- ✎ Are we allowing him to redeem our challenges and create beauty out of ashes?

- ✎ Are we letting God use our stories to be lifelines to others?

Our stories are designed to be lived out in community to demonstrate the love and grace of God. Jesus lived with his disciples. He sent them to do as he modeled. He sent them out to demonstrate what he had taught. Jesus traveled together with people. He did not set up a *Lone Ranger* ministry. He ministered with twelve men and after he had trained them, he sent them out to do the work two-by-two. Later he sent out a larger group of 72 people, also in pairs. Jesus modeled serving, living, and loving in community. God is a God of community. As his creation, we are a connected people. We are designed to do life together. God's plan is for us tell our stories together.

As Christians in the West, our society is focused on living as individualistic, self-reliant people. Our cultural attitude extends into our Christian living and our approach to community. However, we're called to live as witnesses to the community together.

Jesus sent us to "go and make disciples." Often we don't go at all or we go it alone. What does Jesus mean when he tells us to "go"? We, as Christians and churches, tend to read this as "pack your bags and go somewhere else to make disciples." Some interpret it as a one-time mission trip, and others go one week a year, but is this what Jesus meant? While it's true some people go overseas for a short trip or for a lifetime, this calling is not probably God's plan for most of us.

Living our stories together makes for better stories. If Maria had not connected with other Christians who loved God and knew how to help her live out her story, Megan and Mark's story would have had a very different ending. Maria could not live out her story alone. She learned about God's grace and forgiveness through a group of women who loved and accepted her in the toughest of times. Their faithfulness allowed her to accept God's love and faithfulness. Their acceptance of her allowed her to accept God's forgiveness and forgive herself. As a result, she shared acceptance, grace, and forgiveness with others.

Maria lived her story with others when she reached out to families who were dealing with tough times. She connected with others to love people in their times of need. She created a prayer team, a meals team, and cancer care team to come alongside people. She lived out her calling in community. Together they shared a passion for people in need, and collectively they made a Kingdom difference.

There Is No Community without Unity

When we combine our efforts, much can be accomplished. God created us in his image, and he created us for community. We experience life through living and serving in community.

 Why do so many of us try to go it alone?

 Why do we attempt to reinvent the wheel?

 Why do we shy away from connecting with others to do more good together?

The Fall of Man not only brought sin into the world, but it also brought the break down of community. We don't naturally want to put ourselves aside and accomplish much good together.

God is a God of relationship. Adam and Eve were created in perfect relationship with God and for each other. For a while, they enjoyed peace and perfection. They were two people connected in unity until they chose to disobey. This led to disunity with God and eventually among all people. This disunity among people didn't happen immediately. People kept a form of unity while they spoke the same language.

Most of us know the story of Babel. In Genesis 11, people spoke one language, and they were able to work in a spirit of unity. Although they were connected to each other, they were disconnected from God. They ignored God, and made life and worship about themselves. They decided to build a tower to reach to the heavens. Their big mistake was trying to do something together for the greater glory of who they were as individuals and their earthly community without giving credit to and glorifying God. God saw their activity and realized that humans, left to their own devices with the possibility of collaboration, could accomplish much if they really wanted to. Their man-made unity had great capacity.

To stop them from self-destructive idolatry, God confused their speech, and he brought them from unity to disunity. Now they couldn't communicate, couldn't collaborate, and they no longer were able to build the tower dedicated to their own glory. The result was disunity and dispersion. They scattered around their world, becoming strangers, even enemies.

This was now the new normal. What was that like for people who had lived in relative unity and been able to communicate? Were they shocked? How weird to suddenly no longer be able to speak to your neighbor. How many families were broken up? How many friendships were destroyed? Instead of being a community, they were now disconnected. A Babel resident might have thought, *Yesterday I could talk to you, tell jokes, and share about my life. Today, I can't understand you!* How much war and conflict erupted from that incident? Was that God's design? He designed us for unity in community with him. However, the people of Babel made it about worshipping themselves.

Unity without focus on Jesus can lead to the idolatry of self-oriented living.

God never intended for people to be at odds with each other or with him. However, the choice Adam made plunged us all into a self-centered state. The Babel confusion wouldn't have been necessary if humans had kept their focus on God rather than on pleasing and honoring themselves. The disunity was not God's best for humankind, but it was part of his overall plan to reconcile people to himself.

God desires all people to live in relationship with him. This requires reconciliation of man to God. Jesus came into the world to secure the possibility of reconciliation. Even before Jesus, God worked toward reconciliation. He chose Abram as his son. He desired to bless all nations through Abram— later named Abraham. He chose a people to be a light and example to the world. They were to show God's love for the world and bring a ministry of reconciliation. As God's people, they foreshadowed the coming Messiah. Jesus eventually became God's Lamb, slain for all sins, in order for all people to be given the opportunity to be saved from their sins and for a relationship with God.

Connect for the Kingdom

He Prayed for Unity

During Jesus' last days on earth, his concern centered on his disciples. Did they understand who he was and his purpose for coming? They had been amazed at his teaching and his power, but they were confused about his purpose. Jesus lamented several times over their smallness of faith and slowness of understanding. What did he want them to understand? He needed them to fully grasp that he came to reconcile people back to God through his sacrifice on the cross. He was sent from the Father to restore people into relationship with their Creator. He came to liberate people from sin and death to freedom and eternal life.

Jesus clearly told his disciples that his Kingdom was coming, he was the way to the Father, and he came to save the world. In Jesus' last prayers, as recorded in John's Gospel, he prayed for unity and oneness. What would we pray for during our last prayer? I suspect we would pray about the things that were most important to us. What did he pray for? He prayed for unity. He asked God the Father to make his followers one, as he and his Father are one. He prayed:

> So keep them safe by the power of the name that you have given me. Then they will be one with each other, just as you and I are one. While I was with them, I kept them safe by the power you have given me… Father, I don't ask you to take my followers out of the world, but keep them safe from the evil one. They don't belong to this world, and neither do I. Your word is the truth. So let this truth make them

completely yours. I am sending them into the world, just as you sent me. I have given myself completely for their sake, so that they may belong completely to the truth.[5]

He prayed the world would know God sent him. …the world would know Jesus came to reconcile us, his people, to God. As God sent him, he sent his followers. In his final prayer he declared, eternal life is to "know you, the only true God, and Jesus Christ, the one you sent to earth."[6] God sent Jesus to be known and bring eternal life. Eternal life is what we need to be all about and it requires unity.

Jesus wanted his disciples to live in such a way that all people would know they were his disciples. He did not come only to save them, but rather through them bring salvation to everyone.

   How are we to demonstrate the power and love of Jesus? We're to be connected as his disciples and sharing life together in unity and love.

   How are we to demonstrate Jesus' love? We are to tell our stories together so the world may know.

I am not praying just for these followers. I am also praying for everyone else who will have faith because of what my followers will say about me. I want all of them to be one with each other, just as I am one with you and you are one with me. I also want them to be one with us. Then the people of this world will believe that you sent me. I have honored my followers in the same way that you honored me, in order that they may be one with each other, just as we are one. I am one with them, and you are one with me, so that they may become completely one. Then this world's people will know that you sent me. They will know that you love my followers as much as you love me. Father, I want everyone you have given me to be with me, wherever I am. Then they will see the glory that you have given me, because you loved me before the world was created. Good Father, the people of this world don't know you. But I know you, and my followers know that you sent me. I told them what you are like, and I will tell them even more. Then the love that you have for me will become part of them, and I will be one with them.[7]

Jesus paid the ultimate price so we could see who he was, and we could live in relationship with him. Through this relationship, others could come to see the truth and love of Jesus. His purpose was to not only reconcile the few he'd walked with to God, but through them, "everyone else who will have faith" in him.

The Holy Spirit Brought Unity

Before Jesus left his disciples at the ascension, he promised he'd send another Counselor. "Another" as in the same type as he himself had been. Except this new Counselor, the Holy Spirit, was not limited in time and space as Jesus had been while in a human body. This Counselor would be available to all people who believed in and accepted Jesus. He told the disciples to wait for this Counselor.

Ten days after Jesus' ascension, the Holy Spirit was poured out onto the disciples to facilitate their unity as God's witnesses. He came as a rushing wind—mysterious and unpredictable. He came as tongues of fire that separated on the gathered disciples—purifying and holy. He came and gave them the ability to speak in various languages. The Holy Spirit at Pentecost undid the event of the Tower of Babel confusion. He brought unity into the existing disunity. Through him, all those who believed and accepted Jesus could once again be united into one body, one people, and one community and have eternal life.

Jesus prayed for this unity and then provided the necessary person to establish that unity. It comes only through the Spirit of God. We cannot accomplish this unity by our efforts or choice. The unity that demonstrates Jesus' love comes through the power of his Spirit. The Spirit who came at Pentecost empowered the disciples to function as one body and live out the truth and life of Jesus. This same Spirit still resides in believers, and he desires to accomplish this same effect. He still empowers believers to live in unity and demonstrate God's love.

Imagine the possibilities and the purpose of this event. God poured his Spirit into his people. This Spirit unites all believers into one body. Jesus is the Head of the Body. The Holy Spirit lives distributed in all the believers, and we each are a piece of Jesus' body. Together we make up his body.

Only through the Holy Spirit are we connected in unity. And only when we are connected are we the body. Jesus tells us, "Whenever two or three of you come together in my name, I am there with you."[8] It requires more than one of us to make the body.

Jesus calls us to be one church designed to represent God's love and presence on earth. We, as one body, are connected to Jesus as the Head. Jesus wants to live his life through us and bring reconciliation. It's important for each of us to be missionally and incarnationally connected. Together, as a church, we have the ministry of reconciliation. God doesn't need to be reconciled to us. We need to be reconciled to God, which can only happen through Jesus and the salvation he brings. To bring that reconciliation, it's important to live intentionally connected. We're to live in community; each of us connected to other believers.

Live in Christian Community

Why should we be missionally and incarnationally connected? We're to bring people in contact with Jesus in a way that works! Jesus told us that the way to be an impactful community was through love. We're to love each other as he had loved them. He told them, "By this all men will know that you are my disciples, if you love one another."[9] They were to be connected and live a life of love for each other.

Through loving each other, they'd become a magnet to the world.

Jesus wants the same for and from us. As his followers, it's important to connect in love and through loving be united in such a powerful way people notice there is something unique about being a part of a Christian community. This may already happen in our churches—but if it does, this community often occurs behind walls. When we only love each other within the church's four walls, people cannot see how we love each other. We need to demonstrate this love out in the community in authentic and attractive ways.

According to Dietrich Bonhoeffer, theologian and martyr, we're not creating Christian community. Christian community exists by definition because we're part of God's family, and he is a relational God. Community is God's idea. God lives in community. He created us for community. Community exists in Christ. Christian community exists because the Holy Spirit is distributed among God's people. It's a reality created by God in Christ in which we may participate.

Many of us don't have good examples of Christians or the church living out this kind of love. Often, our experiences with Christian community are limited to the rather shallow interactions on a Sunday morning. It's polite, friendly, and unlike any other relationships in our lives. Undoubtedly there are churches that may have deep, caring, and genuine relationships, but for many of us Sunday morning church is not a fun celebration with our favorite friends and family members. In many ways, church gatherings are unnatural and disconnected. Luckily for all of us, Jesus offers more! In Jesus, genuine community is available to us. It's a choice we make and a reality in which we may participate. We only have to choose to live as he commanded.

> Christian community is founded solely on Jesus Christ, and in fact, it already exists in Christ. It is not an ideal which we must realize, it is rather a reality created by God in Christ in which we may participate. It is a spiritual and not a psychic reality in that it is created by the Spirit.
>
> —*Life Together*, Dietrich Bonhoeffer

What Does a Christian Community Look Like?

What could this community look like? It looks like joyful people doing life together. It means developing deep, close connections with some Christians. This community loves each other and shares meals, spends time, knows each other's stories, takes care of each other, prays together, and discusses deep and significant issues. It's about sharing real life—the joys, the hurts, the victories, and the losses.

This can't be accomplished with dozens of people. Jesus knows our capacity to connect is limited. He invested in twelve men as a group, but he deeply connected with three—Peter, James, and John—during his life on earth. Of course, he only spent three years in ministry, and the dynamics would have changed if he had lived a long life. The point is even the Son of God did not have close relationships with hundreds of people. The Apostle Paul invested in a few, such as Timothy, Silas, Titus, and Luke,

> The missional emphasis involves connecting with people where they live and deploying them as kingdom agents in their natural settings and established relational networks.
> [It] also implies an agenda of connecting Jesus followers with each other to engage in an external focus by deploying to serve people in the community.
>
> —Reggie McNeal

and through them, they invested in others. Like these role models, let's connect with people in close community—sharing life, serving together, praying, and getting closer to God.

Let's expand those communities and invest in other people. We can't only hang out with our three favorite people and assume we have answered Jesus' call.

How can we function being connected in our every day life? It involves intentionally living within the margins and structures God has in our lives. Each community might function differently, but it's important that each community be involved in the work of the Kingdom. It's vital for the missional church's focus to be turned outward instead of inward. Let's live connected in a way that people beyond the church can see Jesus and his love. Let's live our stories together, loving each other. We are sent people, so let's live our stories as sent people, and live them together in unity. The community is our close circle of people who we do life with. Beyond our community, let's serve the people God places on our paths—individually and as a connected group—in our neighborhoods, schools, work,...everywhere.

Living missionally in community involves serving together. Jesus came to earth not to be served but to serve. He didn't only sit in a synagogue in Samaria and wait. He didn't place an ad that read, "Missional rabbi opens safe synagogue. Everyone is welcome. Nothing weird. Doors open 24 hours. Come talk to me." Jesus traveled to Samaria and sat on a well. He parked himself at the right time so the Samaritan woman couldn't avoid him. According to cultural rules, he should have maintained an acceptable distance from her, at least twenty feet. He shouldn't have spoken to her, made eye contact, or touched the jar she used to carry water. That wasn't appropriate for a Jewish rabbi. Yet, Jesus met her where she lived and the way she was. As his followers, he expects us to follow his example.

Where Is the "Well"?

Where is the "well" in our neighborhood, work or school? Where do we go to sit? Where do we live in such a way that people will discover who Jesus is? We all are sent. We are to live connected, and we are to serve. Serving others grows us to be like Jesus, and spreads his love and life into the world. People around us will experience life as we serve in community. In community means serving together in community as believers—our intentionally connected community. It also means serving as a community of believers, as part of the larger body, the Church. This service should be together in the community, whether that is far or near.

The focus is on "together." Think about serving together in practical ways. Provide tangible help, such as watching kids, feeding pets, mowing lawns, organizing events, making meals, getting groceries, and things like that. The early church we see described in Acts had its roots in this type of service. They lived authentically and noticeably connected:

> All the believers devoted themselves to the apostles' teaching, and to fellowship, and to sharing in meals (including the Lord's Supper), and to prayer. A deep sense of awe came over them all, and the apostles performed many miraculous signs and wonders. And all the believers met together in one place and shared everything they had. They sold their property and possessions and shared the money with those in need. They worshiped together at the Temple each day, met in homes for the Lord's Supper, and shared their meals with great joy and generosity—all the while praising God and enjoying the goodwill of all the people. And each day the Lord added to their fellowship those who were being saved.[10]

They did life together. They lived in such a way that people noticed. They were well-liked. Their neighbors' response might have been, "We want what they have!" Are our neighbors thinking that about us? Do people notice, and do they want what we have relationally?

If we want people to join us, it's important to include fun and fulfillment as part of our gatherings and our lives. We want to enjoy life, yet fun alone is hollow and not enough. We are designed to live on purpose, and we want fulfillment. Serving together with people we love, in an area of passion, fulfills us. Connecting intentionally is about connecting with others that love what we love, and doing something worthwhile that makes a Kingdom difference in our area of passion. It's great if we can have fun while doing it. Ultimately, doing good and making a Kingdom difference is more fun and fulfilling when we do it together with people we love.

How Can We Live Our Stories Together?

Telling our stories together requires community rooted in God with Jesus at the center and empowered by the Holy Spirit. To have a true impact requires us to consistently spend time with God, grow in our relationship with him, and hear from him what we need for our assignment. Our relationship with God is based on how much time we spend with him on a regular basis.

When we consistently spend time with God, we'll be more alert to the opportunities he places before us. We'll notice what he's up to as we daily meet people who do not know Jesus. There are plenty of opportunities. God will work out who and where. It's his job to save people. It's the Holy Spirit's job to draw people to Jesus. It's our job to be available. Maybe all he wants us to do when we meet people who are far away from God is to pray for them—silently.

As a young driver, I often experienced other cars cutting in front of me. I usually grew frustrated, and at times, I shouted or gestured my disapproval. My reactions served no one…they didn't change the other drivers nor lessen my frustration.

One day, God prompted me to pray for anyone who cut in front of me. It occurred to me that I might be the only person who would pray for them on that day. I started my new approach to pray for those who cut me off. Interestingly enough, soon fewer people seemed to cut me off…maybe I no longer noticed or maybe it goes against the work of our enemy. Like my praying for those drivers, maybe all God wants us to do for a person he places on our path is pray for them. Whether God invites us to only pray or also to act, only he knows what each person needs, and therefore, it's imperative we stay focused on his leading.

Missional connecting is primarily about who we are together in community and letting people observe. It's less about what we specifically do. If we love each other, and if we love them in visible and tangible ways, this will cultivate an environment and experience that may lead them to ask questions. Hopefully, it will ultimately lead them to want what we have chosen and embraced for our lives.

When we live together in authentic community, our lives should exude genuine warmth. When we enjoy life together we can sustain demonstrating Jesus' love for a longer period of time. It's much harder to keep loving other people out there by ourselves. The familiar analogy tells us a single ember quickly grows cold, but embers together keep the fire burning.

- Jesus' mandate to love one another for the purpose of advancing his Kingdom sounds relatively easy, right?

- If it's easy, why do we seem to struggle?

- Why doesn't the world see a connected group of people that loves each other with the love of Jesus?

- Why don't we automatically do this? How can we make it easy or at least easier?

Living our stories together, as a loving community, allows us to more easily reach others with the love of Jesus. Why? It's because people have the opportunity to observe our lives. Our stories, lived together, tell the story. They can see us loving each other and loving our neighbors. Living this way will be a witness and will have an impact. It's the Spirit of God who draws people to Jesus. When people are ready to believe in him, it's evident God has been wooing and drawing them to himself. It's like Megan and Mark who experienced Jesus' love through Maria. Like her, let's be instruments of that drawing. It takes behavior that tastes like honey rather than vinegar. If we taste like honey, we make it easier for God to woo people to himself.

Living missionally isn't easy, but it's achievable. We need to be intentional and practical. Rarely does a person have extra time to give. Most of us don't have time to do one more thing. Let's turn what we're already doing into missional activities. Ask the following:

- What are we doing?

◌ Can we do our existing tasks missionally?

◌ Can we approach the relationships we have with a missional mind-set?

If we stop to get coffee in the mornings, look at it as a missional opportunity. (A good excuse to get coffee!) Instead of rushing past people, we can look at the interactions as opportunities to missionally connect and start building relationships. Then, when the time is right and God is drawing them, we will already have the relationships to initiate the conversations God is leading us to. What if we take an extra 30 seconds and invest it in the person we encounter and invest it for eternity? It's about missionally connecting in community for Jesus. Our efforts will make a Kingdom difference when we live our lives intentionally and stay focused on Jesus.

Who is God putting on our paths today? Even if all we do is pray for the people we come across, lives will change. Jesus will be doing his part and people's hearts will be affected for him.

Living It Out

Let's rethink what it means to be and live as the Church. We know the way. We have the answer. We can provide hope. It'll require us to live as one, just as Jesus and the Father are one. The Trinity lives in perfect unity. We are created in God's image. We're meant for relationship with God and with each other. This unity will be the unmistakable and irresistible witness. People need love. They need hope. They need a solution. It's time to unite, so we can be a living, active, and effective witness of the love of Jesus and his Good News. Ready?

Key Concepts

◌ Telling our stories in community.

◌ We cannot have true community without Holy Spirit unity.

◌ To tell the great news of Jesus, we need to tell our stories together.

◌ It requires community to impact the mission of Jesus.

◌ Each of us needs to live our story intentionally together with others living their stories intentionally.

Questions for Living It Out

1. Do you know someone like Maria? Have you experienced hard times?

2. Are you giving your story and challenges to Jesus so he can demonstrate his love and grace through you? Are you allowing him to redeem your challenges?

3. Who are you living your story with? Who are the people involved in your story?

4. How does God want to deploy your story with others? What is your calling in the context of community?

5. Does your community look differently than that of your neighbors? Do people notice the difference?

6. Where is the "well" in your neighborhood, work or school? Are you hanging out at the well? Where do we need to live in such a way that people will discover who Jesus is?

7. Does the world see a connected group of people that loves each other with the love of Jesus?

8. Are you approaching your life, tasks and relationships intentionally in a missional way? Who is God putting on your path today?

Notes

1. See 1 Peter 3:15

2. Charles H. Spurgeon, "A Sermon and a Reminiscence," *Sword and the Trowel*, March 1873 as cited on http://www.spurgeon.org/s_and_t/srmn1873.htm. Accessed online July 27, 2012.

3. See Hebrews 10:24-25

4. 1 Peter 3:15, NIV

5. John 17:11-19, CEV

6. John 17:3, NLT

7. John 17:20-26, CEV

8. Matthew 18:20, CEV

9. John 13:35, NIV

10. Acts 2:42-47, NLT

Chapter 6

Grow into Your Original Design

Personality is only ripe when a man has made the truth his own.

—Søren Kierkegaard

If you have anything really valuable to contribute to the world it will come through the expression of your own personality, that single spark of divinity that sets you off and makes you different from every other living creature.

—Bruce Barton

For we are God's handiwork, created in Christ Jesus to do good works, which God prepared in advance for us to do.

—Ephesians 2:10, NIV

Two Stories of Personal Discovery

Tom Changes Careers

Tom landed the job he believed he was born to do, but the journey had been a long one with a few detours.

He recalled being sure before, but he had soon realized the career he diligently prepared for wasn't what he wanted to do for the rest of his life! After he had finished college, Tom trained to be an airline pilot and went to fly for a major carrier. He loved flying and was good at his job, but he couldn't imagine working as a pilot until retirement in 30 plus years.

After considerable thought and prayer, Tom retrained for a totally different career, which led to his dream job, working at a Christian financial services company. He loved working with customers and networking—aspects that are a must for a person in business development. He relished the varied aspects of his responsibilities and the contacts he made with people.

Similar to the monotonous summer heat, his curiosity lingered longer than welcome when his mind locked onto the big change in direction he had taken in his career. He prided himself on his ability to focus and his drive to succeed. He knew about his wiring—or so he thought—but he still couldn't explain the total career change.

One day, an opportunity unfolded to discover more about what had changed in his life. When Tom had joined his new company, they invested in his personal growth, as was their policy for all their employees. They wanted to maximize the team's total potential, as well as unleash each employee's personal best to make a difference—not only at work, and in personal relationships, but also as volunteers performing good work in the community.

When Tom was asked to meet with Jenny, the company's executive coach, he politely informed her, "I took the prerequisite strengths, personality, and spiritual gifts assessments. I know who I am." He glanced at his watch keenly aware of his calendar filled with appointments.

Jenny sat across the table from Tom. Her hair was the color of late summer's grass, and she had a pleasant face. She smiled, waiting a moment before speaking, and then said, "That's great. It helps a lot when you understand yourself." Her expression became more serious. "Tell me about your career path."

Tom stretched his long legs in front of him, and dutifully explained how he had changed careers. "I'm a little surprised that I like working business development as much as I currently am."

"You are an extravert and are great with new people! Your personality and strengths made you for this, but it also explains why you were attracted to becoming a pilot," Jenny locked her gaze on Tom as if she was double checking to see if he was tracking with her. She pointed to the results and clarified what prompted his career change. "Your wiring is ideal for your new career, especially in your responsibilities working with existing and prospective clients."

Meeting with Jenny proved to be very helpful and the benefits continued beyond work as his company intended. Finally, Tom found out how to really plug into the community to bring the love and life of Jesus in a way that felt right. He valued integrity and action, but he didn't like routine. God had built him to work with people over a long period of time. Based on better understanding his wiring, he made the decision to mentor young men in his community.

Tom also realized his keen ability to network and build relationships, and he learned how to view his work as a missional opportunity—viewing clients and colleagues as people who need the love of Jesus not only financial services.

As a result of investing in discovering his wiring, Tom now knows how God designed him, and acquiring this knowledge has helped him to discover his purpose. It increased his joy in all aspects of his life. Now more than ever he strives to live each day to make a difference in God's Kingdom.

Victoria Rediscovers Volunteering

Victoria, a woman in her late forties who was built like a long distance runner, was a former church secretary. She loved her church and had given many hours of her time to volunteer in the office. With her years of experience, it was no wonder she knew her way around an office setting better than most.

"Victoria, we really appreciate all your wonderful help," the pastor had told her. Remembering the conversation made her feel worthwhile. His appreciation was why she continued to support the staff.

But discontentment brewed under the surface. Victoria preferred not doing administrative tasks, yet that's where she was appreciated, and that's what the church wanted from her. This inner conflict grew in her life.

When she considered what she loved to do, showing hospitality and having people over to her home, jumped to the forefront. These activities truly gave her the greatest joy. She loved getting the house ready and making people feel cared for. It came easy to her, but she never truly saw it as useful for Jesus' Kingdom.

Victoria's life had been pretty tough, and she spent many years as a single mom. Through it all, she never let her circumstances determine her attitude. She worked hard to put her kids through school. Eventually, she pursued her own dream to become an interior designer. After completing her studies, she started her own business, and she loved helping people make their houses wonderful homes designed and decorated according to their own taste.

Yet, she knew parts of her life did not line up. In her attempt to passionately follow and serve Jesus, she wondered if he was leading her to give up her business. Recently, she had stopped actively pursuing new clients. To fill the void, she volunteered more in the church office.

One day her church held a training event designed to help people find their wiring, focus, and passion. Victoria participated. She took strengths, personality and spiritual gifts assessments. The results provided a new and helpful perspective. She met with, Susan, a coach the church had brought in, who helped her pull it all together.

"You clearly are an extravert, Victoria," Susan had told her in her one-on-one meeting. Her warm smile put Victoria at ease. "You get your energy from people."

"I love being with people," Victoria said, beaming at Susan. She brushed away a lock of hair and continued, "The more the merrier." Her laughter filled the room.

"That's right, but you also need a plan and schedule," Susan added, pointing at the report. "You function best when things are organized and calendared."

"You're so right," Victoria agreed sheepishly. "It's one of my challenges, but I need order." She tapped the table making her point. "What do you think my spiritual gifts indicate?"

Susan looked at her papers, smiled, and said, "Hospitality and service. They are a perfect match for your whole personality and talents." She shook her head laughing. "With your strengths of harmony, and helping people to develop and grow, you are wired for working with people."

"I do love people, and I love to plan and organize," Victoria added, as she leaned her arms on the table.

"You told me you enjoy making people's houses into true homes," Susan paused making sure Victoria agreed and was ready for her assessment. She continued, "You could put all the aspects of what you love to do, your gift of hospitality, knack for design, and love for people, to serve your community with the love of Jesus."

"Really? How?" Victoria asked wide-eyed, leaning closer to catch every nugget Susan may give her.

"With your passion for serving the disadvantaged, especially single moms who have experienced a rough time in life, you could work with a lo-cal housing organization that provides low-income apartments for single moms and their families," Susan explained, lightly touching Victoria's hand. "You could make these basic places a warm and welcoming home! What do you think?"

After thinking it through and covering it in prayer, Victoria decided to put her wiring to work. She would take on one project at a time and work with the women to make their apartments the kinds of homes they would be proud to live in and love to come home to. She would use her gift of design to create a great place. She could use her strengths of harmony and development to work with the women and help them take the next steps in getting their lives back together. She would give them the gift of hospi-tality by creating a place to call home.

Victoria, energized by the possibilities, now sees volunteering in a totally new light. She still occasionally helps out at the church, but her pastor fully supports her new direction. He loves how she passionately helps single moms and deploys her strengths, personality, spiritual gifts, and designer talents to serve people with the love of Jesus. Finding her fit in the body of Christ has given Victoria's life new meaning.

You Are Part of God's Story

God created each one of us in his image and for his purposes. Genesis 1:27 tells us:

So God created human beings in his own image.
In the image of God he created them;
male and female he created them.[1]

God created us as part of his overall plan. He chose us before he created the world—we are chosen to be holy and blameless in his sight.[2] It means: we matter as individuals! We are part of his plan. Given God's view of us, where do we fit in his story, the ultimate story?

The idea of an ultimate story is not in vogue these days. The concept of a metanarrative,[3] an overall story based on universal truth that gives meaning to all our individual stories, has ceased to be the norm. In a postmodern[4] world, people have multiple stories and everyone is left to sort out their version or story. To the postmodern, truth is relative and based on personal experiences. In this worldview, truth isn't ultimate or absolute, but it's based on personally derived meaning, individual experiences, situations, and circumstances. "Faith in the one God who revealed himself in Jesus Christ doesn't fit into the pluralistic postmodern order."[5] This view of truth has become pervasive in the Western world.

Christians know there is an ultimate story—a true metanarrative. God created the universe, and he created sinless people to be in a genuine and mutual relationship with him. His original design was marred by the Fall in the Garden of Eden, and the story took a sad turn. People chose to go their own way, causing a separation from God. Ever since this tragic event, God has been in pursuit of reconciling people back into a loving relationship with him. The ultimate story is one of God seeking to restore people to their original design. This design includes being made in God's image—holy, righteous, and good. Jesus came to restore us to that image. Now those of us who believe in Jesus are made into a new creation—one that is designed to reflect his image. God wants to reconcile all people to himself. His plan includes deploying his children, people who have already been reconciled to him, to reach those who are still far away from him. He knows how he made each of us, and how he wants to utilize us, as his children, according to his design.

As God's creation, each of us contains a very finite aspect of his infinite personality and character. Being made in his image, each person carries a little deposit of God's character and attributes. When we understand that we represent different aspects of God, it becomes clear we need to value those differences. Obviously none of us contain all of God. He gave each of us a piece of the puzzle and a limited view. No one sees all, we only see a tiny slice. As people, we think that our view, our small slice, is the whole picture. We cannot imagine others see it differently because what we see is so obvious to us and it looks complete.

In reality, we don't see the whole—we only see a tiny bit, only our own point of view. And, the more we embrace this truth, the more we realize we need each other to understand the big picture. Only when we unite, as God's people, do we represent more of God's character and attributes. God designed us to connect as a body for his purposes because we look more like God when we're connected versus when we're separate individuals.

What an amazing truth! The God of the universe designed each one of us exactly as he intended. He shared himself with his people. As the Creator, he handcrafted us with unique personalities and placed us in a specific cultural context on history's timeline for his purpose. How can we be sure? God shows us through the stories of his people. As we see throughout the Scriptures, he placed hand-picked people in specific times and contexts.

The Disciples Lived Their Part of the Story

In the New Testament, the disciples provide us with some great examples of this. Jesus chose twelve very different men to follow him and be his disciples. Through their individual stories, we see how the issue of personality and purpose played out in their lives.

The disciple, Andrew, seems to have been a fairly quiet person, but he possessed an inviting personality. He brought Peter to Jesus. We see him bringing others to Jesus too—including the boy with the five loaves and two fish.[6]

Nathanael appears to have been precise. He required facts, and he seemed to want empirical evidence. When Philip told him they had found the Messiah, Nathanael was skeptical. Eventually, Philip persuaded him to come check Jesus out. When Jesus saw him, he said of Nathanael, "Here truly is an Israelite in whom there is no deceit."[7] He was a dot the i's and cross the t's kind of man.

Andrew and Nathanael were very different from James and John. James and John were two brothers who were manly men, and approached life with passion and testosterone. Jesus referred to them as, the "Sons of Thunder,"[8] an appropriate label, as they offered to call down fire from heaven to destroy an uncooperative village.[9]

The Bible shows us more about Peter's personality. We know him as impulsive, extroverted, and a leader. His personality leaps off the pages of Scripture as bold, brash, and courageous at times. Other times, he seems fearful and a bit dimwitted. Peter appears to always have been ready for an adventure. His exploits range from stepping out of the boat onto the water to wielding a sword to cut off an ear. He lived with passion. His heart and his mouth demonstrated great faith in Jesus, but they also caused deep grief. The Gospels are full of examples of Peter's personality!

Thomas seemed more cautious than Peter. He wanted proof of Jesus' resurrection and not hearsay from his fellow disciples. Did he doubt or did he want facts? We don't know, but it's clear, once he was convinced of the validity of Jesus' resurrection, Thomas was totally sold out to Christ's deity and worshipped him.[10]

The brief glimpses we see of the disciples' personalities and character clearly reveal that each of the twelve brought a distinct approach and style to the group. Jesus chose them, and he knew them. He did not treat them as if they were all alike, but he clearly allowed for their differences. In John Chapter 21, while restoring Peter, he made it evident he had specific purposes and plans for each disciple. When Peter asked him, "Lord, what about him?"[11] Jesus told him, "If I want him to remain alive until I return, what is that to you? You must follow me."[12]

Jesus knew their unique character traits and personalities. He treated them as individuals, and he sent them out according to who they were.

He still does that with us today. Jesus came to set us free from sin and death. We are free to be all God designed us to be. Understanding and embracing this truth is exciting!

We Have Our Part in the Story

Jesus intends us to live into our design and use it for his Kingdom. The Apostle Paul taught about the importance of bringing our differences together for God's purposes. In Ephesians 4, he writes we are to "live a life worthy of the calling"[13] we have received. It's key to bring our unique designs to Jesus and allow him, through his Holy Spirit, to blend us into one body. "There is one body and one Spirit, just as [we] were called to one hope when [we] were called; one Lord, one faith, one baptism; one God and Father of all, who is over all and through all and in all."[14]

It is about unity in diversity. Paul continues to explain that God has given each one of us grace as Christ apportioned it.[15] Jesus gave different gifts and assignments to people, based on how he created each one, "…so that the body of Christ may be built up until we reach unity in the faith and in the knowledge of the Son of God, and we become mature, attaining to the whole measure of the fullness of Christ."[16] Jesus is the head, and we're the parts of the body. He holds us together, and we, as a body, are "joined and held together by every supporting ligament" that "grows and builds itself up in love, as each part does its work."[17]

Our assignment is just that—our assignment—within the larger assignment. When we zoom out, we see the bigger picture. On our own, we see just one small piece. It is important to do our part well because it's what God gave us to do. Our part is valid and important for us to do, but it's not more important in God's Kingdom than someone else's part. Our part is the most important for us to do because it's what he made us to contribute to his bigger plan and purpose. Let's remember, we're part of the whole but not the whole. We each bring our unique part to the body. Therefore, it's important for each of us to find our function and not copy someone else's role or approach.

Lincoln Brewster, singer and guitarist, spoke about being fully who God intends you to be at the 2009 National Outreach Convention (NOC). He led the worship for the entire event, and he made the point to each of the attendees that we should embrace our uniqueness!

Lincoln Brewster told of his early experience in serving in a church worship band. He came from the band, Journey, and he had experienced the lavish but unfulfilled life as a rock star. Now, he had found Jesus and wanted to serve him. He spoke to his pastor and soon found himself playing back-up guitar in the worship service. He played the way he thought he was expected to play.

One Sunday, he let loose and rocked out. He surprised the pastor, and the gathered church, when he played his heart out. Afterward, he apologized to the pastor. Luckily, this man encouraged Lincoln. He told him not to apologize, but be himself, to let loose and play his heart out for God. That's what he has been doing ever since. Now he is "Lincoln Brewster" who gave us such worship songs, as *Today is the Day*. When he played the way God had gifted and wired him, his electric guitar brought worship to God and led others into worship. Lincoln Brewster allowed God to use his gifts, and the church at large has been blessed because of his uniqueness.

God selected, David, the shepherd, to be king over the nation Israel. He loved God, and he tried to serve him. One day, his father sent him to bring some supplies to his brothers on the battlefield. While there, he noticed Goliath ridiculing the Israelite army and blaspheming God.

David was indignant with Goliath's actions and words, and he decided to take action. He approached King Saul who tried to put him in his own armor. After all, you need armor when you go into battle. David tried it on, but he felt like an impostor. So, he went as himself armed with a sling, five smooth stones, and confidence in God's deliverance. We know the story. David served the way God designed him and God used it to defeat Goliath. He surrendered himself and his wiring to God for his use and glory. The same is true for each of us. It's important to surrender our full self to God.

Jesus has a plan. He created us as he intended, and he made us for his purposes. Our design is intentional. Often we might feel like we need to fit into a box. God did not make us to fit in a box. He made you *you*, and me *me*. We each need to be the best self we can be—for his purpose and glory.

It's important we don't leave our best self at the door of faith and be less than we are, only to keep the peace or gain approval of others. Let's honor the Designer and his plans for each of us. Let's live into his purpose and into our design. Let's embrace our uniqueness for his glory.

You Are the Only You We Will Ever Have

Most people want to do good works, but we may not fully know who we are and what God has for us to do. We want to know God's will for our lives. As we've discussed, God specifically designed us, and we have a God-given purpose. Our personality, strengths, talents and gifts are as God intended them to be. We're his original masterpieces.

God made no reprints or copies. We truly are one-of-a-kind and exclusively designed. There never have been two people exactly alike. God has made each one of us distinct and true originals. Ephesians 2:10 tells us that we are God's workmanship, his poem.

Grow into Your Original Design

How do we embrace our God-ordained design? What are we supposed to *do*? What is God's will for our lives? What is our purpose? How can we make our lives count?

> You are a slave to Christ, an ambassador of God, a servant of the King, a soldier in the invisible battle of purity and evil. You will find inner peace only when you know who you truly are. Only at that point can you be authentic.
>
> —George Barna

Living into God's purpose and design for us requires us to grow—both personally and spiritually. God has a master plan for each of us, and he will provide the opportunities for us to grow into his original design for each of us. To become all we are designed to be, God will challenge us to know and love him, to follow his call for us, and to authentically live out our lives as he leads.

Know and Love God

Key to making our lives count is to know God and grow in our relationship with him. Spend time, every day, in prayer with God and in his Word. Learn to know God, develop a deep relationship with Jesus, and be filled with the Holy Spirit. A genuine and growing relationship with God is imperative to living a God-filled life on purpose for his Kingdom. As we grow in our relationship with God and seek to follow Jesus, we will come to know his best for us. As we love and obey him, we will grow in spiritual maturity. As we mature, we will be able to respond to his purpose for our lives.

Growing spiritually also entails healing emotionally. Spiritual growth and emotional health go hand in hand. Why? Loving God fully entails our heart, mind and soul.[18] An injured or unwell heart, mind, and soul will affect our relationship with God.

When we grow spiritually, God will illuminate areas of our lives that need attention and healing (if we let him). And, as we heal, we'll have greater capacity to grow in our love and relationship with him. Growing spiritually affects our emotional health. Healing our hurts affects our spiritual maturation. The deeper our relationship grows with God and Jesus, the easier and safer it is to explore our hurts and tender areas. The more secure we are in God's love, the safer it is to explore those areas that need healing. Everyone has hurts and emotional dents. Once we decide to let God get into the messy areas of our soul, he will set us on a path of greater emotional health. Healing leads us to freedom, which allows us to hear more about what God has in store for us and who he wants us to be in Jesus.

Follow God's Call

Another element of making our life count is knowing and following God's call on us today. Some of us might know what his ultimate call is on our lives, but many of us live our everyday lives without a sense of God's greater purpose or true call. Author and Spiritual Director, Ruth Haley Barton, wrote in her wonderful book, *Strengthening the Soul of Your Leadership*, that God's call is, "First and foremost the calling to be yourself, that self that God created you to be."[19] She points out God is calling us to be the individuals we were born to be. One way to discover his call is to look at what brings us deep gladness and a sense of meaning. Ultimately, calling is about our relationship with God and becoming all that he created us to be. We are called to fully be who we were made to be… according to God's design. We can only realize the meaning of our lives if we rise to our full purpose of our being here on earth.[20] We will only be truly fulfilled and find real meaning when we live into our full potential and answer God's call.

God calls all his children to be and do according to his purpose and pleasure. Our job is to say, "Yes" to God. Let's be about the people and tasks he puts on our path. Let's do what our hands find to do for his glory. God calls us to go and live out our faith. He wants each one of our lives to bring honor and glory to his Name. One way to answer the call for today, while preparing for what God might ultimately have in store for us, is freeing ourselves to live into how we are designed. He wants us to live a life that brings glory to him and to grow.

> *…in the New Testament portrayal of mission the central reality is the active work of the living Holy Spirit himself. It is the Spirit who brings about conversion, the Spirit who equips those who are called with the gifts needed for all the varied forms of ministry, and the Spirit who guides the church into all the truth.*
>
> —Bishop Lesslie Newbigin

Live as the Person God Made You to Be

We know God originally created human beings in his image with great potential. As part of creating us, he gave everyone potential. We have potential because we are all image bearers of God himself. Potential speaks of what could happen, but it's not a guarantee of development. Potential requires nurturing.

When I started kindergarten in the Netherlands, my teacher believed in my potential. With a November birthday, I missed the cut off and had to wait an extra year to begin elementary school but that did not stop her. She thought that with a little help from my mom, I could catch up and skip a grade. I greatly benefited because my mom invested in me and spent the time to teach me to read and do basic math. Consequently, I skipped first grade making me the youngest in my grade from then on out. Being the youngest was fun, but being appropriately challenged and not bored was the true gift.

In college, while attending Santa Clara University in California, a math professor spotted potential and invested in me. My math knowledge was below standard, and my grades showed it. He saw I could do well enough with a little extra tutoring. Professor Dave Logothetti challenged me to dig deeper and I passed Calculus and Trigonometry, which were prerequisites for my business degree. All it took was a person who helped me use my potential.

When I began my career in public relations, my boss, John Tsantes, recognized my potential, and he urged me to grow in my profession. As a vice president in our high-tech agency, he spent hours explaining PC boards, semiconductors, and CAD, in order for me to be able to write white papers and press releases for my clients. He coached me, so I could represent my clients well in conversations with editors of technical magazines.

When I began pursuing writing, David Kopp challenged me to focus and develop the craft. (Hopefully his hard work paid off!) He encouraged me to keep writing. All of these people invested in the potential God placed in me. Their efforts made a difference.

God wants to develop the potential he gave each of us, not only for our regular lives, but for our eternal lives. God will invest in us and bring out the best, in order for us to be what we were created to be. Our part is to show up and to apply intentionality, skill, and training.

Learning more about who we are, what we are best at, and what we are meant to do helps us discover true joy in life, relationships, work, and volunteering. Each of us is created for this time and place with one-of-a-kind wiring, which can be uncovered and honed so we can enjoy greater success in our daily life and in our service to God. God will do in and through us all he intends when we show up prepared.

Preparing ourselves for action requires us to get ready for God's plans for and in us. In *What's So Spiritual About Your Gifts*, Dr. Henry Blackaby advocates asking, "What does God want to do through me?" rather than, "What can I do for God?"[21] We might wonder what kind of tasks God has intended for us when the right question for us to ask is, "What kind of me" does God want for his mission? Growing personally requires us to become fully ourselves—that self God created us to be. Only then, will we be ready for the tasks God has for us to do.

The Apostle Paul discusses the fact that God's people have specific assignments.[22] We as the church, are a body, and like the human body, each part has a role. The roles are different, but every part is needed. Paul encourages us to serve as we are wired—to do our part as part of the body. If a hand attempts to do the work of the foot, two people are displaced. The foot does not have its task and the hand is poorly equipped for "foot work."

God values each person, and he has given people distinct callings. Pursuing personal discovery to find our fit, as part of the body, is biblical and useful for effective work in the Kingdom. What better way than to know our gifts, personalities, and strengths, and those strengths of the people around us in order to bring God's hope and love as the whole church to a hurting world?

Most of us hunger to make a difference and to have an impact. We long to belong and to find our fit—to discover our unique role. How can we find our fit? How can we find our purpose and easily deploy it for God's Kingdom? How can we be all God wants us to be?

Discover Your Wiring

One major key to discovering God's purposes and design for our lives is by learning how he made us. What is our wiring? How do we think? What are we uniquely good at? What is our approach? What are our preferences? What is our spiritual job description?

Your wiring is worth discovering because God took the time to make you. If we invest in developing our wiring then we are better prepared to fulfill God's purpose for us—for the role he designed for us to play. The role that suits us because he especially prepared us, and the works he has for us to do.

Exactly like Tom and Victoria experienced, when they discovered how they were made, it can powerfully change our life, work, relationships, and service in God's Kingdom. They used strengths, personality, and spiritual gifts assessments to discover details about their wiring. We can too.

Several personal discovery tools[23] exist that can be used to help us discover our distinct design for use in God's Kingdom. These inventories and assessments are not prescriptive, but merely a means to aid in the discovery of God's specific design. The assessments give us language to understand and discuss how God has wired us. As James put it in his letter, "Every good and perfect gift is from above, coming down from the Father of the heavenly lights, who does not change like shifting shadows."[24]

God has given us every talent, skill and ability. It's up to us to discover and develop them. To develop them we need to know what they are. The assessments will allow us to know what God has given us in order for us to develop them—adding skill and knowledge to hone our God-given gifts, talents, and personality into usable tools and strengths.

Personality

God has given each of us our personalities. He intended those to be used for his purpose. He also intends for us to surrender our personalities to him to be shaped and refined, so we're more like Jesus in our attitude and behavior. However, God doesn't want us to abandon our personalities and become a vanilla version of ourselves in order to become a generic "Christian person." We need to fully be ourselves so God can live fully through us. He wouldn't have given us unique personalities if he meant for us to suppress them! I believe God intends for us to live fully as ourselves, our redeemed selves, with our personalities under Jesus' leadership.

Strengths and Talents

Besides our personalities, God has also created us with strengths and talents—things we are naturally good at. Instead of trying to do something we're not really good at or fixing our weaknesses, God has wired us with natural capacity he intends for us to develop for our own good and for his purposes. If we give him our talents and strengths, he can use it for his

Kingdom. When we focus on our strengths, rather than worrying about fixing our weaknesses, we'll be more effective in life and in ministry. Using our strengths means doing what we are naturally wired to be good at—spending more time on doing what we do best. When we focus on our strengths, it provides us a better opportunity for success. This isn't worldly or material success, although that might happen also, but true success—the success that comes from fully becoming all we can be and accomplishing that purpose in life we were designed to do. Living according to our strengths will also lead us to greater joy because we will like what we're doing. It will be life giving instead of life depleting.

Embracing our talents and strengths allows us to more effectively live in every aspect of our lives. Why? Because when we live according to our strengths, we're free to be our true self, the self God created us to be. When we live this way, it allows us to more fully enjoy what we're doing. Understanding our natural wiring helps us to realize why we respond to certain situations, what motivates or excites us, and how we can make our best contributions.

By discovering our true selves, and by understanding that each of our strengths and talents are tailor-made for us, we'll also realize others are uniquely created. This realization allows us to appreciate our own uniqueness, as well as appreciating the differences within our family, group, or community.

When we know and live according to our strengths, we can love the life we live and develop a true appreciation for the variety God created within the Church and the world around us. We can give to ourselves and others the gift of better understanding. We can also celebrate each of our unique contributions to our community and God's Kingdom. Together, we can bring more strengths to the "team." Each of us can be about what we do best and leave other tasks and responsibilities to team members according to their fit.

Spiritual Gifts

In his writings about the gifts of the Spirit, the Apostle Paul makes it clear that the Holy Spirit intentionally distributed his gifts to each member of the body. Paul explains, "Now to each one the manifestation of the Spirit is given for the common good."[25] The Holy Spirit's gifts are given for the common good, and he distributes them as he determines. I believe spiritual gifts are aspects of the Holy Spirit—he distributes "parts" of himself to the believers so together we reflect the Spirit in us. No one contains his entirety or the fullness of who he is—but the body as a whole receives more or all the facets of him. When we live in unity and deploy the gifts entrusted to us, then we can "see" God's Spirit. As Paul wrote, there are many parts but one body.[26]

Every Christian receives gifts from the Holy Spirit, but no one gets all of them. Scripture teaches that the way we are gifted is meant to be used in and through the local church. Each Christian is designed to be part of a local body of believers (whether church, house church, missional community, or small group) and is gifted (and located there) to build up the body. When we, as local churches, live together as the Church (whether locally or globally) people have the chance to see, know, and experience who Jesus is through the manifestation of the Spirit's gifts.

Spiritual gifts are part of God's spiritual job description for each one of us. These gifts equip us to serve him, contribute to his Kingdom, and be part of building the body. When we use our spiritual gifts, we are effective in the work of the Kingdom and the result to us is joy. God's gifts to us are to be used for the common good, but they also benefit us. We feel fulfilled and receive joy when we exercise our gifts as part of the Church.

Find Your Passion

When we truly live into our personality, use our strengths and serve according to our gifts, we exercise our wiring to its full potential. Deploying our wiring does not make all of life's problems disappear, but it enhances our joy and effectiveness. When we embrace who we truly are, we discover it is OK to be ourselves. In God's plan, we are supposed to be ourselves!

There's only one of each of us, and it brings honor to God when we become the best self—surrendered to him and his purpose—we can be. I'm free to be fully me for his purpose and glory. You are free to be you for his purpose and glory.

For many of us, part of truly living for God's purpose and glory means finding our passion. What is our passion? Often it relates to what upsets or annoys us.

- What irritates you?
- What is your soapbox?
- When you see injustice, are you ignited to right certain wrongs?
- Maybe inefficiency and duplication of effort annoys you, as it does me.
- Maybe seeing hurting children makes you want to make a difference.
- Maybe the loneliness of so many elderly distresses you.

The possibilities are endless. I know my passions relate to my pet peeves—somehow I am motivated to invest my time and energy to fix or alleviate the things that bother me. This is true for many of us. Often our passion relates to the things we want to improve. Other times, it relates to experiences we've had that we want to use to help others.

Get into Focus

When we know our wiring, our calling, and our passion, we are ready to focus on what God has for us next.

- Maybe it means growing our character or going deeper into our relationship with God.
- Maybe it means putting what we've already learned into action.

Knowing how we are wired, and what we are passionate about, will only make a difference if we put it to work. It will not make a difference if we neatly place the information on the shelf.

The purpose for growing into our original design is putting it into action. Let's focus on the people and tasks God has for us to do. He will want to use our wiring—including personality, strengths, and gifts—to accomplish the good works he has for us to do. Our job is to bring our prepared self to God, so he can utilize us to complete the works he hand-designed for us.

I love Edith Wharton's quote, "There are two ways of spreading light: be the candle or the mirror that reflects it." Jesus is the candle. We're the mirror when we focus on him and reflect his light. Each one of us is a unique mirror. Let's shine his light into the community in the way he intended, and in the place he placed us. Our wiring helps us to reflect the light our way. Each of us uniquely reflects the light—and it's a necessary part of the whole. It requires everyone contributing his or her part to reflect the prism of Jesus' light.

Discovering our wiring and understanding our passion is not enough. It's important to focus on what God has for us to do, and then for us to complete our assignments. The Apostle Paul writes to the church in Colosse to tell Archippus, a worker in God's Kingdom, "See to it that you complete the ministry you have received in the Lord."[27]

Let's focus on understanding ourselves in order to complete the work. God created us for the work he has for us to do.

Put Your Best Self into Action

God created us as unique members of his body. He wired us for relationship with him. Based on our wiring, he prepared good works for us. When we understand our wiring and show up prepared, God will use us in his Kingdom.

Working and serving God according to our wiring brings us joy and fulfillment. It answers the "Why am I here?" question and gives us purpose. Eric Liddell was a Christian and a runner—his story was told in the famous movie, *Chariots of Fire*. He explained, "I believe God made me for a purpose, but he also made me fast. And when I run, I feel his pleasure." Liddell understood his wiring, passion, and purpose. What is our version of running? What makes us feel his pleasure? How do we prepare—as a runner prepares? I believe we need to:

Be ready:
Let's be spiritually formed and committed to growing in maturity, skill, and knowledge.

Know and be our true self:
Let's discover and understand our wiring—including personality, strengths, and spiritual gifts.

Know God:
Let's invest in our relationship with God, spend time with him, and truly get to know him based on his Word.

Be part of the Church:
Let's live out who we are in and with a community of Christians.

Find our fit:
Let's discover our unique calling—the works God has prepared for us to do.

Get equipped:
Let's invest in our wiring so we truly understand who we are and what we can do. Once we understand our wiring, let's get equipped (adding skill and knowledge), so we can be most useful in God's Kingdom.

The Apostle Paul describes the Christian life as a race. He writes, "In a race all the runners run… Run in such a way as to get the prize."[28] For us to put our best self into action, it's important to be like athletes who prepare for a race. Let's get fully equipped to run the race marked out for us.

Living It Out

Reggie McNeal says, "God is always up to something new."[29] Where is God heading in my life and your life? Let's follow Jesus into the community and look at where God is already at work. God's word to each of us is, "Be you!"

We can't walk in someone else's shoes. David couldn't be David in Saul's armor. Being our true self is the only way we can live and have our lives tell our part of God's story. Let's focus on being the best self we can be according to our calling and in our context.

Be you. Do what you are designed to do. Let your life tell the story.

Key Concepts

- ☙ God uniquely created us, and he has a plan for us.

- ☙ Let's become all God created us to be according to our wiring.

- ☙ To embrace our design, let's grow spiritually and personally.

- ☙ Let's discover and invest in our wiring—our personality, strengths, gifts, and passion.

Questions for Living It Out

1. Have you embraced your God-ordained design? Have you discovered your unique wiring? Have you taken personality, strengths, and spiritual gifts assessments?[30]

2. Do you know God's will for your life? What is your purpose?

3. Do you have a plan to spiritually grow? To personally grow? Did you have a plan but have you stopped working the plan?

4. Do you know what God wants to do through you? Have you asked him?

5. How can your wiring help you live out the love of God in community?

6. Where is God leading? Are you joining him there? Who does he need you to be, to do what he has designed you to do?

Notes

1. Genesis 1:27, NLT

2. See Ephesians 1:4

3. Metanarrative simply means a "big story." A metanarrative is a theory or grand story that seeks to provide a total, comprehensive account to explain history, events, experiences, culture, and social phenomena based on the adherence to a universal truth or values. The Biblical metanarrative is the big story about God.

4. Postmodernism is a reaction to modernism and, in general, rejects universal truth and all-encompassing explanations of facts and meaning that apply to all people and cultures. Postmodernism focuses on the relative truths of each person, placing high value on interpretation. Truth is not absolute but rather a construct of the mind as it tries to understand its own individual and personal reality.

5. David J. Bosch, *Believing in the Future: Toward a Missiology of Western Culture* (Valley Forge, PA: Trinity Press International, 1995), 44.

6. See John 6:8-9

7. John 1:47, NIV (Entire passage John 1:45-51)

8. See Mark 3:17

9. See Luke 9:54

10. See John 20:28

11. John 21:21, NIV

12. John 21:22, NIV

13. Ephesians 4:1, NIV

14. Ephesians 4:4-6, NIV

15. See Ephesians 4:7

16. Ephesians 4:12-13, NIV

17. Ephesians 4:16, NIV

18. See Matthew 22:37

19. Ruth Haley Barton, *Strengthening the Soul of Your Leadership: Seeking God in the Crucible of Ministry* (Downers Grove, IL: InterVarsity Press, 2008), 77.

20. Ibid, page 83.

21. Henry T. Blackaby and Mel Blackaby, *What's So Spiritual About Your Gifts?* (Colorado Springs, CO: Multnomah Publishers, 2004), 11.

22. See 1 Corinthians 12:12-31

23. As a StrengthsFinder advisor and Myers-Briggs coach, I like to use the Gallup StrengthsFinder and Myers-Briggs Type Indicator tools. I also use an online spiritual gifts inventory. Contact me at henriet@TheStoryLives.com or visit TheStoryLives.com for more information.

24. James 1:17, NIV

25. 1 Corinthians 12:7, NIV

26. See 1 Corinthians 12:12-14

27. Colossians 4:17, NIV

28. 1 Corinthians 9:24, NIV

29. Reggie McNeal, Warm Beach Camp, November 2006.

30. For information about the assessments I use or learn more about how to discover your wiring send me an email at henriet@TheStoryLives.com or visit TheStoryLives.com

Chapter 7

Live a Life of Meaning

As a prisoner for the Lord, then, I urge you to live a life worthy of the calling you have received.

—Ephesians 4:1, NIV

No one is useless in this world who lightens the burdens of another.

—Charles Dickens

Henriët's Story

For as long as I can remember, I've wanted to make a difference with my life and in the world. My desire to make a difference has always included God.

Keenly aware that we all only have one life to live, I wanted mine to count for God. From my earliest recollections, he was a big part of my life. Even as a child my heart was intent on learning his purpose for me.

It Started in the Netherlands

Somehow, by God's grace, I knew him despite growing up post-Christian in the Netherlands. My family wasn't particularly religious, but my parents believed in God, and we attended church about ten times a year. Faith in God was part of our lives. For me, God was definitely real, and I never doubted his existence. He answered my prayers. I talked to him, and I talked about him. Even in a culture where people didn't discuss

God, I spoke about him. God took part in my daily life so talking about this reality in my life seemed, well—normal. My childhood with loving and faithful parents, helped set me on my life's course—the course God intended for me.

When my sister and I were little, my mom faithfully read the children's Bible to us. We grew up with faith but not religion.

When I was sixteen years old, my family moved to the United States. As a teen, this was a huge culture shock. Luckily, I had already met, Fred, a great guy—the man I would marry just two years later—who helped me, and my whole family, transition. Fred helped us adjust not only to every-day life in California, but he also helped us in our relationship with God in this new culture. He was an authentic Christian who lived his faith. He was the first guy I had ever met that not only had an interest in, but also a relationship with God. We both desired to live lives of purpose.

Fred took us to a great church he attended every week—Peninsula Bible Church (PBC) in, Palo Alto, led by Pastor Ray Stedman. We loved this real church that taught Scripture. Under Pastor Stedman's teaching, and the teaching by the entire pastoral team at PBC, I began to really learn the truth about Scripture, and the responsibilities and requirements of a Christian life—including reading the Bible, praying, attending a small group, and participating in evangelism. These disciplines and practices helped me to grow in my knowledge and relationship with God.

Growing in my faith increased my desire to lead a meaningful life. I longed to invest my story for Jesus. I learned living for Jesus meant shar-ing my faith. Even with all the growing and learning, the idea of sharing the Gospel remained very uncomfortable. The process other Christians explained seemed awkward and difficult. The idea of asking strangers and friends if they knew Christ and then leading them to a place where they prayed to accept Jesus seemed so foreign! I lived with the kind of guilt that lay heavy on me like a hot, wet blanket.

Jesus said that if anyone is ashamed of him and his words that he will be ashamed of that person too before his Father and the angels![1] The last thing I wanted to do is displease Jesus but witnessing in that way seemed too weird. After much consternation, I found a way to deal with it—I focused on Christians and discipleship. After all, helping people to grow in their knowledge and relationship with Jesus is a worthwhile endeavor too, right? Periodically I still felt a little guilty, but I mostly tried to put it out of my mind. I poured my life into helping people to spiritually heal and emotionally grow. I led Bible studies, discipled people, and stepped into leading women's ministries and small groups.

God Called Me

During the time at PBC, I remember thinking that it would be much easier to share about Jesus with people if I was a pastor. One Sunday morning, during a sermon, this thought really struck me. One of the pastors at PBC, Ron Richie, would tell stories of how people would engage him in conversation, which led to him explaining about Jesus. In one sermon, he mentioned how he got gas for his Datsun 240Z at a local gas station. He struck up a conversation with one of the attendants, and they talked about various things. When he was finished filling up, and the gas cap had been put back on, the attendant said, "Richie, one of these days you'll have to tell me what you do for a living." Richie smiled and agreed—one day. After this visit, he continued building the relationship by meeting with the attendant. He eventually explained not only what he did, but he told him about Jesus.

During that story I very explicitly thought, "I wish I was a pastor. Sharing about Jesus would be natural and part of everyday life." Of course that day passed, and it was a rogue thought. In my context, women did not become pastors.

Years went by—probably about five or six years—and I mostly forgot about the sermon and my thought about becoming a pastor. I worked in public relations at a small local agency, attended church with my husband, and we joined a small group. We had left PBC and were part of Lincoln Glen Church, a smaller church closer to our home. I had become involved in leading women's ministries, and we attended Sunday school.

One day, a fellow leader asked me to attend a half-day of prayer. I'd never heard of such a thing and certainly had never prayed for such a long period of time. This event sounded strange, and I had no desire to spend time in prayer for three hours! I planned to ignore the request and let it pass. The leader persisted, and eventually cornered me. Finally, I agreed to attend this event.

Per the instructions, I brought my Bible, notebook, and pen. We started with a corporate time of sharing and prayer, then spent two-and-a-half hours on our own...praying. I read my Bible, prayed down my very long list, took a walk, worshiped using a hymnal, and eventually sat quietly in the sunshine filtering through the church foyer's full length windows.

During this peaceful time, a very unexpected thing happened. God spoke to me in my thoughts. He said clearly, "I'm calling you to become a pastor to women and to go back to school."

My eyes opened wide, and I nearly jumped out of my chair. I physically trembled. God was speaking to me! Eager to make sure that I had correctly heard God, and I wasn't talking to myself, I asked for two confirmations.

Having grown up Christian Reformed, I knew that women were not supposed to become pastors. PBC did not have women as pastors. (So my thought back then during Ron Richie's sermon wishing to become one was odd.) At the Mennonite Brethren church we attended, they didn't have women pastors. Mennonite Brethren neither licensed nor ordained women. Yet, God chose to call me to become a pastor at this place. I asked for two confirmations both of which were answered within 28 hours. When God spoke to me, I physically trembled for two hours. Instead of going home, I drove to our senior pastor's home, and I told him what had happened.

My pastor listened, and then he said, "It's a clear call from God. Let's see how we can make this happen."

His response was remarkable and an additional confirmation of God's purpose for my life. My husband, Fred, also affirmed the call, which was important since without it I wouldn't have been able to respond to God's call.

Thus began my new way of life! This prayer event and call happened in April 1989. I quit my job in July, started school in August, and in September of that year, I volunteered on the pastoral staff as pastor to women at Lincoln Glen. I continued focusing on discipling Christians.

Becoming a pastor didn't automatically lead me to share my faith like Ron Richie did with the gas station attendant and others. Over the years, I'd fallen into the way church was "done," and I had forgotten my desire to share Jesus with people outside the church. I focused on those inside, and only had the occasional opportunity to invite people to put their faith in Jesus. Every conversion excited me, but my focus and ministry occurred inside the four walls of the church. After all, that was my "job" as volunteer pastor.

After four years, we moved to Washington State where we found Timberlake Christian Fellowship, a Free Methodist church. Timberlake employed ordained female pastors. I volunteered my time, and after the pastor of adult ministries encouraged me, I pursued ordination and joined the church staff. Things were going well for me as a staff pastor, but again I grew restless.

I Rediscovered My Roots at Fuller Seminary

Then in 2005, I attended Fuller Seminary, and enrolled in the Master of Arts in Global Leadership through the School of Intercultural Studies. In my studies, I learned much about church, missional ministry, and outreach. We learned about the changing paradigm in churches from seeker to missional. During those studies, I rediscovered my roots. As we studied about modernism and postmodernism, Christendom and post-Christendom, I realized I had grown up in a postmodern and post-Christian culture in the Netherlands.

This shift from modernism to postmodernism and Christendom to post-Christendom, now has been happening in the United States. In learning about postmodernism, post-Christianity and missional ministry, I reconnected to my missional roots. One day, while working on a class project, I recalled how, as a kid, I'd shared openly and easily about God and my relationship with him. I also recalled how in my PBC days, a desire began to percolate—the desire to be a pastor and to share about Jesus. Most significantly, I learned sharing Jesus in today's world required living missionally in an intentional way. It meant living rather than telling your story—sharing Jesus' love naturally as part of daily life. It required a different approach, but the same approach I had used when I was in elementary school!

Returning to my roots and relearning missional living excited me. I knew how to have conversations and build relationships. Understanding missional ministry connected the dots. Now I could fully live according to Jesus' calling. Living missionally gave my life the added meaning and allowed me to witness naturally—bringing honor and glory to God.

> *The Great Commission entrusted to the church was to go into all the world, not to beckon to the world to come to it. The Good Shepherd does not stand by the gate of the sheep pen calling for lost sheep to return but goes out in search of lost sheep.*
>
> —Eddie Gibbs

One Life to Live

We all have one life to live. How will we live our one life? Who will we influence for God's Kingdom?

In the area where I live, the majority of people will never attend a Christian church. Never! This fact is astonishing. This means most of the churches trying to bring in "seekers" are "competing" for a relatively small percentage of the people in the area.

This concept captured me, and led me to think in a different way. What about the majority of unreached people? Didn't Jesus specifically concern himself with those people—the ones who are disinclined to attend any church? If so, how did he live? How did he seek to reach the unreached? What does his approach mean for us?

As we discussed in Chapter 3, *Observing Jesus' Story*, Jesus lived his story among the people…including those who did not attend church. He met the woman at the well. He touched lepers. He sought and met people, instead of waiting for them to approach him. He didn't sit in a local synagogue saying, "I'm here and available if anyone wants to talk about God or salvation." The Gospels give us many examples of how Jesus interacted with everyday people in everyday life.

Reggie McNeal helped me see this reality in a new way. At a retreat he led,[2] he retold the story of the woman at the well.[3] He explained how

Jesus sent the disciples into town, but he stayed at the well. The disciples were on a mission to buy bread and missed this woman and the others—probably even avoided them. Jesus intentionally sat and waited where the woman would walk to the well with her water bucket. He intentionally sat and waited at the well in order to speak to her.

This meeting changed her life, and it eventually changed the lives of the people in her town. McNeal explained that the church acts more like the disciples than Jesus. We, as church people, are busy going to town to take care of our ministry needs and miss the people on our path. In his book, *Present Future*,[4] he addresses the need for the church to become missional. Ultimately we, as the church, are sent to get out there and meet the woman at the well.

At the retreat, McNeal also said that, "God is always up to something new." So old ways and repeating the tried and true do not necessarily help us to bring the Good News of the Kingdom of God to people in need of Jesus today. As Christ-followers, let's keep our eyes on God and be ready to follow him into the work he's doing around us. This may very well require doing something new. As the church, our focus is to look outside and getting involved in the community. McNeal talks about the need for new scorecards. Instead of measuring attendance, buildings, and cash, we need to count missional conversations, intentional encounters, and acts of service. We need to live outside the box and demonstrate God's love in new ways.

How do we reach the majority no longer looking for God in church? Perhaps it's important to think about ways other than putting on a better show on Sunday mornings or adding to our church ministries.

This new focus (new emphasis) requires us, as Christians, to live missionally in an intentional way.

Desire to Live on Purpose

Once I thought through this paradigm shift, my eyes opened and my heart changed. My focus emerged to reach the unreached but not in any traditional way. I was relieved that being missional and sharing Jesus didn't ask me to buttonhole people, share an evangelistic tract, and get them to pray the prayer all in one sitting. I realized I had to live in a way that made a difference in people's lives. This was the way I had lived as a kid in the Netherlands. With God's help, I could live missionally and intentionally again!

God had always been and continued to be real in my life. It was now important to learn again to demonstrate God's presence in my daily life. I had figured it out in some of my friendships—and being a pastor definitely helped. They knew what I did, therefore, I could talk about God, offer to pray for them, and in other ways demonstrate the truth of God in my life. However, I grew discouraged, as it never seemed to lead these friends to attend church.

During a conversation with a British friend, he asked me, "What's the value-added benefit for me if I come to church on Sunday?" I could not answer that question! He and I regularly talked about God. He believed in God, did not really know Jesus yet, and he didn't live his faith in any noticeable way.

His question to me was, "What would Sunday morning add?" The way Sunday services worked I couldn't give him a solid answer that made any sense. I sat in my office and sadness swept over me. For weeks, my inability to express the value of attending church haunted me.

This experience led me to again look at things in different ways. God led me to crystalize my thinking. Most of my neighbors, friends, and people in the community weren't looking to attend church. My approach didn't depend on making the right "ask" or figuring out the right program, ministry, or message to invite them. People weren't looking for church nor were they looking for God in church. They were barely looking for God at all.

There had to be a better way to reach these great people with the Good News of Jesus.

  ⌖ What would this better way be?

  ⌖ How could I live differently to show how Jesus made the difference?

Daily Live Your Story for Jesus

God began to make "the way" obvious. Again, Reggie McNeal helped to bring clarity. During a class he taught at Fuller,[5] he elaborated on the need for a new approach. He told stories of talking to servers in restaurants, baristas in coffee shops, and clerks in stores. He struck up conversations and demonstrated interest in their lives and concern for their struggles. If they shared needs, he'd ask if he could pray for them. The people he engaged in conversation never refused to let him pray for them. He wouldn't necessarily pray for them in public, but he definitely included them in his regular prayer times.

One day, Reggie offered to pray for a young man who had significant struggles and no relationship with God or background in church. When Reggie asked if he could pray, this young waiter stopped and bowed his head right there in the restaurant. Reggie McNeal realized that this young man thought he would pray right then and there, and he did! This man didn't know as Christians, we offer prayer, but we don't necessarily mean right then and there. Reggie asked this young waiter if he could pray for him, and he assumed that this would be now. This waiter didn't know enough to "know better." How refreshing. I love this story. It illustrates people are open to the love of God, and they aren't preprogrammed against him. We only need to be open to what God is doing, and how he wants to use our lives to make a Kingdom difference. Reggie created opportunities for relationship and conversation with the people he interacted with. He developed connections of trust, and people began to share their lives, ask for prayer and even express interest in Jesus.

Could it really be this easy? A group of us went out to dinner one night after the class, and we tested Reggie McNeal's approach. We struck up a conversation with our waitress. She shared she was moving and had concerns.

We asked her if we could pray for her. She smiled and said, "Yes," and we prayed for her on the spot. It works! When she opened her eyes, a tear slid down her cheek and she said smiling, "Thank you guys! That was nice. I think I already feel a little better." We were thrilled and promised to continue praying for her. That was it! She cleaned the plates and went back to work. We decided to get dessert.

I thought hard how to sustain the implementation of this approach in my life. My questions were:

- How could I intentionally invest my life to make a difference for Jesus?

- How could I interact with people in real life and naturally share about Jesus as opportunities came up?

One of my first steps was to explore and understand my own wiring. My goal was to genuinely live out my life in a way that was sustainable. For me, it meant visiting a friend whose husband had cancer, opening my home to my son's teenage friends who had no place to stay, and other opportunities that showed up as part of daily life. It also meant being alert to friends and family, and looking for opportunities to pray or offer tangible help whenever possible.

All of this made sense because I had lived this way before in the Netherlands, though I did not necessarily pray or offer help back then. I just talked about God to people. I talked about him as a person. He was real to me and was part of my everyday life. There had been little to no resistance to it back then. Now I resumed that practice with great intentionality. People want to be loved and cared for. Nobody minds it if you pray for them…if it is without church strings attached.

Share Jesus' Love

One of my friends connected me with a colleague whose dad was dying of cancer. I visited her dad in the hospital. He was rapidly losing the battle against esophagus cancer. Fear was reflected on the man's face. We talked about faith. I regularly visited him until the day he died. He had professed knowledge of Jesus, and my prayers seemed to comfort him. After he passed away, I was invited to attend the service at the cemetery and conduct a special family service at the home of one of the relatives. WOW! They invited me to pray and give words of hope to a grieving family who had no connections to God or to church. Nobody prayed to receive Jesus on that day, but I had an opportunity to be Jesus to about twenty people.

A few years ago, a friend's mother died. She asked me to do her memorial service. Her mother's friends, neighbors, and colleagues attended. Most did not know Jesus. I shared stories about my friend's mother and told them about Jesus in a relational way. People heard about God. Nobody received Jesus that day either, as far as I know, but people were introduced or reintroduced to him. What a great way to demonstrate the love of Jesus. Some of my friends jokingly call me the "last chapter pastor" because I enjoy helping families with the last part of life and conducting memorial services. Why do I like it?

ᓚ It is a great place to tell the story of Jesus.

ᓚ I'm able to love people during one of the hardest times in their lives.

ᓚ I'm able to demonstrate the love of Jesus. That is exciting to me!

Intentionally living on mission with Jesus allows me to make a difference. I am investing in the people that God places on my path. I don't have to look very far for opportunities. I only need to be alert to God's leading in my life. Who is he sending for me to touch and reach out to? Sometimes it's a one-time touch. Other times there are ongoing, longer-term relationships. Either way, it's God who leads me to and through these opportunities.

God is faithful, and I love when he chooses to use me in a missional way. However, I am not faithful. Unfortunately, there are many opportunities that I missed or did not show up for. Sometimes I disobeyed, other times I allowed myself to get too busy, and there were all those times of distraction. Living missionally isn't difficult, but it's best to leave room for God and commit to following his lead.

Investing our lives requires:

ᓚ allowing for margin;

ᓚ paying attention; and

ᓚ being intentional.

It means being aware of where God is at work in our life and in the lives around us. This does not have to be stressful but needs to be intentional. God will lead us; we only have to pay attention. It's up to God to lead us.

Jack Deere, author and pastor, says it's about Jesus leading us more than it's about us following him. He writes, "Put your confidence in his ability to lead you, not in your ability to follow."[6] God doesn't depend on us to correctly follow. Jesus will lead us if we keep our eyes on him.

The ideas and insights about living missionally began during my time at Fuller. My classes and reading helped me to think about what's required to truly show God's love. People aren't waiting for us to tell them about Jesus. They're not looking for church. Most of them are just living their lives.

The times that people are most receptive to experiencing Jesus is when they are in need. When their lives hit some snag or even a crisis, they are often more open to experiencing the love of Jesus. However, it means we have to develop relationships with people before this happens.

Being there for people truly presents an opportunity for the Gospel. It opens a door for us as we seek to share Jesus with people. If we intentionally look for opportunities to do good work, we can incarnationally demonstrate the truth and reality of Jesus.

Live as Sent Ones

Clearly, the Gospel is meant to be shared, and to share it requires us to live as sent ones. The Gospel is the Good News that has freed us from slavery and death, and it allows us access to God and the ability to live without fear of death or slavery to sin. How amazing! People need to hear this news. The Christians' armor includes the shoes of the Gospel of Peace.[7] These "shoes" allow us to stand secure! We can stand when our life is based on the truth of the Gospel. Wearing these shoes, we can stand and travel as soldiers of Christ. With our armor on, we can move out with God's great news, confident in sharing the Gospel.

How do sent ones live? They are people who understand Jesus' love for them and others, and who want to share this love in meaningful ways. Sharing Jesus' love shouldn't be an obligation, but rather it should be a joy and privilege flowing out of our relationship with him. How this works out for each person depends on their individual wiring, individual situation, and the context God has placed them in.

What is our purpose, our wiring, and our focus? (For more on this refer to Chapter 6, *Grow into Your Original Design*.) Understanding our wiring will help us naturally live out Jesus' love. Living as sent ones, means living the way we are wired within the context of our life to reach others with the love of Jesus. It might mean helping out a neighbor, praying for a teacher, buying a cup of coffee for the person in line behind us, starting a conversation with the grocery clerk, learning the name of our favorite barista or food server and asking them about their lives…the possibilities are endless. Maybe it means choosing to show interest in our colleagues in the workplace. Maybe it involves praying for those in our neighborhood.

Living as sent ones allows us to respond to our context based on our wiring, passions and God's calling on us. If we give who we are to God, he will use us to demonstrate his love through us. He will deploy our wiring, gifts, passions, and life experiences to his honor and glory. He will invest our lives for his Kingdom and bless us with spiritual growth and blessings in Christ. As Paul writes God, "…has blessed us in the heavenly realms with every spiritual blessing in Christ."[8] Jesus tells us that when we put God and his Kingdom first God will take care of the rest.[9]

How would this work? Where can we find these opportunities to love our neighbor? Besides, paying attention to people in our every day lives and investing in the people around us, one simple way to live like sent ones is to intentionally connect with existing local volunteer opportunities. This can be done by helping out at a local nonprofit organization that works in an area of interest that we are passionate about. Volunteer opportunities are great ways to be the hands and feet of Jesus.

This is especially true when we volunteer in order to demonstrate the love of Jesus. People can experience Jesus when we serve them or work with them. Giving a little time weekly, monthly, or occasionally, and getting to know the people we serve, or serve with, will create opportunities to demonstrate Jesus' love. It will also provide connections, which will give us an opportunity to pray for people and their needs. This approach allows us to put our wiring and passions to work in a simple and meaningful way.

Live a Life Worthy of Your Calling

God wants us to live our lives in a way that allows him to show his love for others. He wants us to let our stories touch others with his love. It doesn't require moving to Africa or Asia. (Though it may for some.)

Living a life worthy of our calling requires:

   ❧ willingness to be open to the people around us;

   ❧ investing some time in their lives; and

   ❧ offering God's love—whether through prayer, through tangible help, or both.

Investing our stories requires us to live a life worthy of the calling.

In the New Testament, there are many verses, which talk about living such a life. As Christians, let's live a life that responds to God's love and Jesus' sacrifice for us. I deeply desire to live a life worthy of the Lord Jesus, a life of meaning. After my life on earth is through, I long to hear, "Well done, good and faithful servant!"[10] To hear those words, I'll have had to invest my life according to the calling I've received.

What does this kind of life look like? Why should we strive to live this way? In Ephesians, Paul urges Christians to live a life worthy of the calling because we've been called by God.[11] Living a worthwhile life requires us to realize that we have been bought with a price.[12] We're not our own. Therefore, we need to live the life that our Master, Jesus, wants us to live. During his last days, he was explicit with his disciples. He wanted them to:

   ❧ obey his commandments;

   ❧ love God and each other; and

   ❧ live in unity and rely on the Spirit.[13]

He said obeying his commandments involved loving God and loving each other. Jesus considered this kind of love so important that he made it the litmus test of true discipleship. Why? He made it clear, loving each other as he loves us is the way people will recognize us as his disciples.[14]

Part of a meaningful life entails making disciples and helping Christians grow deeper in their relationship with God. To take people deeper, it's important to continue growing spiritually in Jesus. It requires maturing to mature others. As we grow deeper, we'll be better equipped to make more and better disciples. When we connect with other Christians, let's intentionally do life together—this means loving each other, loving God, and being the Church with and to each other. It means growing in our relationship with God and with each other. In Acts 2, we see a picture of the Church living like this model. The disciples regularly gathered, shared everything they owned, and no one had need. Christ-followers lived a life worthy of their calling and were noticed by the people around them.

Living a life of meaning also requires surrender. If we belong to Jesus, then he is the Lord of our lives. Living a life of meaning means:

- Jesus is on the throne of our lives and we obey him.

- We surrender our hopes, dreams, talents, time, money, and our wiring to him for his purpose and glory.

- We give our lives to God for him to transform. He wants to grow and change us to be like Jesus.

What kind of life pleases the Lord? Paul succinctly tells us that living a life that's pleasing to God will require us to be careful how we live. "Don't live like fools, but like those who are wise. Make the most of every opportunity in these evil days. Don't act thoughtlessly, but understand what the Lord wants you to do."[15]

Living a life of meaning also requires us to act. Let's do what he tells us to do. Jesus tells us to:

- go and make disciples;

- love one another as he loved us;

- stay rooted in him so he can produce fruit through us; and

- actively live our faith.

As God's people, let's live in such a way that demonstrates our faith. We can't authentically agree with the verses in the Bible without living them out. It's important to actively demonstrate our faith. James writes, "…faith by itself isn't enough. Unless it produces good deeds, it is dead and useless."[16] Our love and faith should flow into good deeds and produce fruit. As James says, "If you are wise and understand God's ways, prove it by living an honorable life, doing good works with the humility that comes from wisdom."[17] As children of God, let's use our money and time to do good for others. Let's be rich in good works and generous to those in need, always ready to share with others[18]—both inside and outside the church.

According to Paul, a life worthy of Jesus involves certain behaviors and characteristics, including being humble, gentle, and patient. Paul tells us to, "Be patient with each other, making allowance for each other's faults because of your love."[19] We need to be kind, tenderhearted, and forgiving—just as Christ forgave us.[20] It means growing in maturity, speaking the truth in love and becoming more like Jesus, the head of the body, his church.[21] When we interact with each other, we need to live a life of love. According to Paul, those who live this way will tell the truth, not let anger control them, be sexually pure, not use bad language, not be bitter nor angry, not be slanderous nor harsh, nor be part of any other type of evil behavior.[22]

Let's love our fellow believers in Christ. The Apostle John says it this way,

> Dear friends, let us continue to love one another, for love comes from God. Anyone who loves is a child of God and knows God. But anyone who does not love does not know God, for God is love. God showed how much he loved us by sending his one and only Son into the world so that we might have eternal life through him. This is real love—not that we loved God, but that he loved us and sent his Son as a sacrifice to take away our sins. Dear friends, since God loved us that much, we surely ought to love each other. No one has ever seen God. But if we love each other, God lives in us, and his love is brought to full expression in us.[23]

Living a life of love extends beyond our Christian family. It includes our neighbors and people around us. Even when we interact with our enemies, let's exhibit this same love. Being like Christ means living and loving like him. He loved sinners. He involved himself with the people around him and demonstrated God's love to them. As his followers, he told us to love our neighbors[24] and our enemies.[25] He explained to his followers during the Sermon on the Mount that they were to let their good deeds shine brightly in their lives for all to see.[26] Why? So that everyone would praise God.

The Apostles heard him well. Later they write the same message to the churches. Peter writes, "Be careful to live properly among your unbelieving neighbors. Then even if they accuse you of doing wrong, they will see your honorable behavior, and they will give honor to God..."[27] This is how the new church behaved in Jerusalem. In Acts, we read that thousands came to believe in Jesus when they experienced or observed the love of Jesus' followers.[28]

> *Anyone who knows Jesus Christ as Lord and Savior must desire ardently that others should share that knowledge and must rejoice when the number of those who do is multiplied. Where this desire and this rejoicing are absent, we must ask whether something is not wrong at the very center of the church's life.*
>
> —*Bishop* Lesslie Newbigin

Ultimately, living a life of meaning brings honor and glory to God. It's a life of unity and love lived as a testimony to God's goodness. Living this life means keeping the unity of the Spirit and the bond of peace.[29]

Living It Out

Whether we live it out amongst neighbors and friends, or through volunteer opportunities, the important part to remember is to live our lives as *sent ones*.

To live a life of meaning requires us to invest our lives in God's Kingdom. Jesus' major command to us is to make disciples. He saved us, and now he sends us to share his amazingly good news. Let's put on our shoes and make a difference with the one life we've been given.

Key Concepts

- Invest your story and live intentionally missional.
- Live missionally daily within your context and according to your wiring. Be *you* intentionally and share Jesus' love.
- Live a life of meaning to bring honor and glory to God and to reach others with the love of Jesus.
- Live as sent ones and share the Gospel with your every day life.
- Invest in the people around you or volunteer locally.

Questions for Living It Out

1. How did Jesus live and reach people with God's love? What does that mean for you today?

2. How can you help reach the majority that no longer looks for God in church? Are there other ways to bring the Good News?

3. How are you investing your life intentionally to make a difference for Jesus? How can you interact with people in your every day life and naturally share about Jesus?

4. Who is God placing on your path to touch and reach out to?

5. What does living a life worthy of the calling entail? Why should you strive to live this way?

6. Are you living as a sent one? How are you finding opportunities to love your neighbor?

Notes

1. See Luke 9:26

2. Reggie McNeal, Warm Beach Camp, November 2006.

3. See John 4

4. Reggie McNeal, *The Present Future: Six Tough Questions for the Church* (San Francisco: Jossey-Bass, 2003).

5. McNeal, Reggie. Aug. 6-10, 2007. *Missional Leadership: Character, Context and Challenge.* Fuller Theological Seminary, Pasadena, CA.

6. Jack S. Deere, *Surprised by the Power of the Spirit: Discovering How God Speaks and Heals Today* (Grand Rapids, MI: Zondervan, 1993), 199.

7. See Ephesians 6:10-17

8. Ephesians 1:3, NIV

9. See Matthew 6:33

10. Matthew 25:21, NIV

11. See Ephesians 4:1

12. See 1 Corinthians 6:19-20

13. See John 13-17

14. See John 13: 34-35

15. Ephesians 5:15-17, NLT

16. James 2:17, NLT

17. James 3:13, NLT

18. See 1 Timothy 6:18

19. Ephesians 4: 2, NLT

20. See Ephesians 4:32

21. See Ephesians 4:15

22. See Ephesians 4:25-31

23. 1 John 4:7-12, NLT

24. See Matthew 22:39

25. See Luke 6:27-28

26. See Matthew 5:16

27. 1 Peter 2:12, NLT

28. See Acts 2:42-47

29. See Ephesians 4:3

Chapter 8

Partner to Tell the Story

We cannot expect the world to believe the Father sent the Son, that Jesus'
claims are true, and that Christianity is true, unless the world sees some
reality of the oneness of true Christians.

—Francis Schaeffer

Believers are never told to become one; we already are one and
are expected to act like it.

—Joni Eareckson Tada

The more fractured we are, the greater we become spectacles to the world.
The more we are united in love, the more the world sees Christ.

—Curtis C. Thomas

A Tale of Two Partners

The Local Church

City Community Church saw itself as a cutting edge church, involved in the community and committed to be a light to their surrounding neighborhood. Their goal was to grow their people to be maturing Christ-followers. They wanted people to serve either at church or in the community. They had a good children's program, a great youth group, and life-changing small groups for adults. They provided care ministries, and they had missional ministries—mostly giving money to overseas opportunities.

City Community was a good church, but lately they didn't seem to be growing much. People seemed apathetic, and there was a sense of a pervasive status quo. The church staff tried to put a good spin on things, but they were struggling with figuring out what kept people from plugging into the life of the church.

Pastor Tim preached solid sermons, and he regularly encouraged his people to find their fit. They had brought in ministries to help people to do so. The trend was discouraging. He had hoped his leaders would take charge of some of the areas. He had invested in several of them, met with them, set them free to start ministries, and encouraged them to help him lead the church.

Some leaders expressed reluctance, and others only looked the other way, not responding to the need. On average, the statistics for City Community were like every other church: twenty percent of the people do eighty percent of the work. The rest seemed to mostly ride the pews—even though their pews were comfortable chairs. Nevertheless, most sat. He knew many people served in the community, but there was no way to tell who, how often, and in what types of ministries. He had tried to set up a community ministry, but it hadn't taken off either. To say he was drowning in discouragment would be an understatement. Luckily, he was sure of his call to the ministry. He prayed God would show him the way, lead him and his congregation, and bless their church.

His phone rang which brought him out of his reverie. His assistant told him his appointment was waiting for him. He had learned of a local group of churches and nonprofits connecting to do more good together, and had scheduled a meeting with, Kaye, one of the group's leaders.

He smoothed his thining hair, straightened his tie, and strode to the door, holding it open for the tall, thin woman wearing white slacks and a blue, silk blouse walking toward him.

They shook hands, and he invited her to sit at a round table in his office. He joined her.

Taking in a deep breath and slowly releasing it, he hoped exhaustion wasn't reflected on his face.

"How are you today, Pastor Tim?" She smiled.

"Life is full." He tried to pump some energy into his voice, but he knew he failed in the attempt.

Kaye laughed. "I use that euphemism when the stuff on my plate is larger than the time in my day. I understand." Then she sat quietly for a moment, as if she was studying him. "Pastor Tim, I've been on your side of the desk. Church work is hard. People mean well, love the Lord, and they expect you to run a perfect church. They expect you to feed them on Sunday, entertain them during the week, take care of the kids, challenge their youth, care for their sick family and friends, and provide meaningful service opportunities, have an active mission program, and vital small groups all without enough staff or enough money." She stopped to take a breath. "Of course, a good number of members want all of this, but they don't want to donate toward the budget. After all, it's not exciting to pay for light bulbs."

Pastor Tim smiled, "Your assessment reflects some of my job on any given day, but please know I love my congregation, and I've got good people here. They are people praying for me and my work."

Kaye nodded. "If you could have whatever you wanted, what would it be? Would you want to have a ministry to the community without adding to your workload? Provide opportunities for people to serve and have a way to know what they are doing in the community? Create greater visibility for your church? Would you want to energize your people so they are more excited about your church, bring their friends and give more of their money?"

For a moment, Pastor Tim fell silent, clasping his hands. "It all sounds good. I'm sure we all want that." He settled back. "Our vision is to grow more and better disciples, and for us to be a light to the community. I'd like people to be excited about that."

Kaye smiled again. "It's a great vision. What if there was a network of partners who wanted to help you make that happen? Would you be open to collaborating in a community to help you achieve your vision?"

Pastor Tim leaned forward. "I'm always looking for ways to live out the vision and mission of City Community."

Taking his answer, Kaye explained that the local group of churches and nonprofits partner to help each other achieve their vision to reach the community for Christ by providing easy pathways for service, and opportunities for connecting with other Christians. She added that the benefits to the church were many, including creating greater visibility in the community, and enhancing people's commitment to the church through participation, outreach, and even giving.

After the meeting ended and Kaye left, Pastor Tim grew more intrigued with the concept of partnering—and, he wanted it to work. This group saw itself as a missional partner—relieving him of the stress and guilt of providing missional opportunities in the community in isolation, as well as the pressure of keeping another program going.

He signed up his church to join the local partner network and announced it to the people of City Community. He was excited he could provide his congregation with choices of either community-based volunteer opportunities or those originated through City Community programs.

His breathing was once again slow and steady. He was pleasantly surprised to learn Brandon, one of the leaders in his congregation, had been involved with this partner network, volunteering in the community. He loved being active in the network. Brandon told him how he had found them through receiving an invitation from a mutual friend to participate in a volunteer opportunity. He explained he had been serving ever since, using his executive skills for about six months and loving his work.

Pastor Tim allowed himself to dream for a moment, and to imagine City Community people volunteering with their neighbors, impacting the community, being excited about the opportunities, and bringing that excitement back to the congregation on Sundays.

Over the next few weeks, Pastor Tim told his City Community congregation about new ways to be involved in the surrounding community. He brought in people from the network to share the various opportunities. He had always talked about the value of neighbors and the importance of being an integral part of the community.

The Local Nonprofit

Jonathan House, a safe hangout for teens, started by a young man who understood the need for safe places, recently received additional funding. Things were going very well. Of course, they could use more volunteers.

Pam, the director, sat behind her desk, and shook her head. *Interesting how everyone wants to have a safe place for teens, but it seems virtually impossible to find people willing to volunteer, mentor, and tutor. How were these teens supposed to find their way, have a safe place if it was just more of the same—a hang out without loving supervision, spiritual and moral guidance, and ways to make sense out of their confusing world?*

She stared at the pile of paperwork and list of unanswered phone calls, and it was only Monday morning. She needed a shift supervisor, a doctor, some health counselors, a math tutor, a 'cool' science tutor, some grandparents to tell stories and mentor the younger teen boys and girls, and some 20-somethings to be cool and provide peer mentoring. The list went on. She could also use a CFO and an operations person to give her some advice and some marketing help. She smiled, in spite of her exhaustion. A wry smile.

Where would these people come from? Most people didn't even know Jonathan House existed. And, it really didn't seem like people cared much about these teens—except warehousing them as a tidy solution.

She turned on her desktop and checked her email. She chose to ignore the state of her desk—she'd have to deal with the mound of chaos later. An office manager would be nice too.

She sighed. *Dream on, Pam.*

Scanning her emails, her eye caught a notice from one of the churches that periodically helped with lunches. The subject line intrigued her: "Partner network provides leaders, mentors and volunteers to community organizations." She leaned against the back of her chair. "City Community Church has joined with a local group to provide tailored opportunities to volunteer in the community." *How does that work? I hope I don't regret this.* She hestitated, and then clicked the link included in the email.

She sent an email, and not long afterward, she received a reply. Clearly, these people understood her needs as a nonprofit director. She needed trained, committed people, but she had no bandwidth to recruit, train, and retrain. Her success and ability to fulfill her vision depended on a team of willing and able volunteers.

Pam released a long sigh of relief after she joined the network. She now had partners to provide better services to the community! Tears welled up in her eyes and spilled onto her cheeks—tears of relief and gratitude. For the first time in a long time, she didn't feel alone. There were other people who cared about her community. Others who loved teens. Others who understood her passion, her heartache, and the difficulties of what she was trying to accomplish.

Six months later, she had several new, committed volunteers: some grandparents, a counselor and John. John was a regular donating one morning a week to help her run operations. He was a CEO of his own small business and understood how to run an organization. Pam knew it was working because her own desk looked a lot more peaceful. In fact, she could see the color of the wood again. A good sign! These last few months helped her to remember why she wanted to get involved in this work in the first place. She loved what she did again. She had not been able to say that in a long time. She had been too tired, overwhelmed, and discouraged.

What if This Tale Was True?

Pastor Tim and Pam's stories reveal the possibilities when people and organizations work together. When we work together, we do more good in the community. It also benefits people inside organizations because they feel connected to the larger cause. Partnering connects them and provides resources. None of us are designed to do it all or by ourselves. Harry Truman said it well, "It is amazing what you can accomplish if you do not care who gets the credit." So if we can do more together and everyone benefits, why don't we do it? Or, why don't we do it more often?

There are various answers, including our systems, theologies, and practical hinderances. Our church and nonprofit systems keep us inside the box of our own making. We're busy and so committed to the vision, mission or just our job, we can't look beyond our own four walls. Sometimes our view of God and Jesus keeps us from working together because we have theological differences based on our interpretation of Scripture. We also can be convinced our visions, missions, and callings vary too much to work together. Additionally, work takes too much of our time and energy so that we don't have the bandwidth to look across the street or develop relationships with organizations across town. Working together sounds easy, but sometimes making it work becomes difficult.

When I served as pastor of adult ministries, my responsibilities included community involvement along with the more typical tasks of that role. My team worked to connect people with local ministry or mission opportunities. We also wanted to celebrate what people in our church were doing in the community. Sounds simple enough, right?

In my experience, both aspects of this responsibility proved to be difficult. I found there are no easy pathways to connect people with opportunities in the community. We wanted to help our church attendees connect with existing nonprofit volunteer opportunities to be the Church in the community—in practical and tangible ways. The concept seemed simple, but making it happen proved too challenging, and we never got this part of the work off the ground. It left us sad and dissatisfied.

I love the idea of being the body together and serving the community, not only as a local church, but as churches partnering to demonstrate Jesus' love. My passion is to see Christians, churches, and nonprofits *be* the Church, serving the community together. I'm not alone in this passion. Currently, many people and churches are returning to Jesus' original plan of a united church. The Apostle Paul wrote that Jesus is our peace and destroyed the dividing wall of hostility.[1] All people who follow him are one.

The Church Is a Witness to the World

Living in Unity Points to God

Jesus prayed for unity in his last recorded prayer before his suffering, death, and resurrection. He also told the disciples living a life of love for God, and for each other, would demonstrate this unity to the world. He wanted his followers to live in unity with him, and the Father, so all people might come to see and know the one true God and Jesus Christ whom he had sent.[2] It is a powerful witness the Holy Spirit uses to draw people to Jesus. When his people live in unity, it demonstrates the Gospel lived out.

What does a community living in unity look and act like? The Apostle Paul describes it this way:

> As a prisoner of the Lord, I beg you to live in a way that is worthy of the people God has chosen to be his own. Always be humble and gentle. Patiently put up with each other and love each other. Try your best to let God's Spirit keep your hearts united. Do this by living at peace. All of you are part of the same body. There is only one Spirit of God, just as you were given one hope when you were chosen to be God's people. We have only one Lord, one faith, and one baptism.[3]

As Jesus' followers, let's do the following:
- Love each other.
- Be kind to and gentle with each other.
- Work to keep our hearts united.

The goal is to actively live as parts of the same body, which demonstrates:
- We belong to the one God.
- We have one Lord.
- We share one faith.

Luckily, Jesus did not require us to do this on our own. After he prayed for unity, he promised to send the Holy Spirit. It's the Spirit's job to bring this unity and to help us to live united in him.

What does this mean for us?

We are to cooperate and be one! One body, living out one faith, guided by one Spirit, being one Church to demonstrate we belong to one Lord who is over all.

Why?

It shows the world the truth about Jesus. The world is divided, but the body of Christ should be united. Our unity and love should set us apart so people can see Jesus.

Together in unity we, his people, represent Jesus to the community.

Let's live a life of love and demonstrate God's love for people.
Let's be Jesus in action.

Living in unity is difficult. God created each of us as unique creatures. We are different, and those differences provide both the spice and challenges of life in relationships. It takes effort, humility, and most of all the Holy Spirit for us to live in unity. Why? It requires putting the community before our individual needs. Living in unity is not the norm and not the way of the world. Jesus called us to unity for an important reason—so we can reflect him to a watching world.

When We Live as Reconciled People We Draw Others

Jesus came to save people from their sin and to reconcile them to God. He came to save a broken world. His purpose wasn't to save everyone when he was on earth. Rather, he chose to use his followers to demonstrate his love and power. He sends us to this broken and lost world. We need to be about reaching the world with the love of God. Jesus came to reconcile people to God. He wants people to be reconciled to their original state and design—to be in communion and relationship with him. Jesus is the way to this reconciliation. People are in need, and they need Jesus.

How can we reach the world with Jesus' reconciliation? Through active love lived out in unity.

The Father sent his Son Jesus to reconcile the world to him. Jesus came to earth and died so we might have life. He loved us so we would love God and each other. He plainly told us people would come to know him if we loved each other—like he loved us. It is about the unity of our witness as his people. As Jesus' followers, we need to bring the ministry of reconciliation. This requires us to live as Jesus' body, the Church—together. Living as a community of love, unified by the power of the Holy Spirit, is the reversal of Babel.

When we live together, love each other, love God, and actively love our neighbor, the world will see, hear, and experience that Jesus still is the Savior of the world. Living life this way demonstrates he loves us and them. It provides the living proof he wants to reconcile all people to himself.

Therefore, to be the Church and to be true witnesses to a watching world, it's importnt to live in unity. Jesus knew the only way we would advance the Kingdom, and be agents of reconciliation, is through unity.

Unity requires:
- the Holy Spirit;
- our surrender to the head of the body;
- our willingness to think about Jesus, and his Kingdom, rather than ourselves and our turf; and
- putting ourselves aside and working toward the greater good.

It's countercultural. It's what is needed right now.

People need good news now maybe more than ever! The world is a scary and dark place. The economies across the globe are faltering. There are massive natural disasters. Many countries are dealing with political unrest. There no longer is a metanarrative that even many Christians believe to help them make sense of it all. Many of us hold onto a worldview influenced by the world rather than by God. Even God's people often are uncertain. People need Jesus—both Christians and non-Christians.

The world truly is in need of good news, not bad news. Many churches and Christians have been witnesses to a weak Gospel without good news. How is it good news if we look like the world? How are we different if Christian organizations look and act like secular organizations—competing and protecting turf? How is it good news if we cannot even get along with each other? Who wants to be part of that kind of faith or church? Are we surprised we are losing ground?

People can only receive the Good News that Jesus loves them, died for their sins, and came to give them life, when we, his followers, live in such a way that it truly seems like good news!

They can better hear and believe the Good News when we love God, love each other, and love them with the love of Jesus. We can have the greatest positive effect when we look like one body, and we collaborate in love for the sake of the Kingdom to reach the least of these. Jesus prayed for us to live in unity. He told his followers to love one another and show a united family, a Church. And do we? I think the answer is "No!"

> *The issue is not to talk more about God in a culture that has become irreligious, but how to express, ethically, the coming of God's reign, how to help people respond to the real questions of their context, how to break with the paradigm according to which religion has to do only with the private sphere.*
>
> —David Bosch

How Is the Church Doing?

We've Behaved Badly

It seems obvious that throughout the ages the Church at large, and local churches (in general), have not always lived in unity and demonstrated love. In recent decades, the Church and Christians have been seen as judgmental, critical, unkind, and exclusive. We now have a bad PR problem. Thanks to our own actions and lack of demonstrated love, we have a well-deserved bad image. We are perceived as infighting and not getting along. What a tragedy! How this must grieve Jesus who came and died so we might have life—and live as witnesses to this life!

One of the problems we face is a divided church. We are divided on issues, theology, and practice. The list goes on. People outside the church body don't understand this division.

I imagine them asking the following questions:

- Don't you all believe in the same Jesus?

- Don't you all believe in the same God?

- Aren't you all Christians?

- Why don't you all get along?

Sometimes non-Christians get along better with each other than Christians do! How confusing is that? It's confusing to me, and I belong to the church. How much more confusing is it if you are not part of the church? We really have behaved badly. We haven't lived in unity. Our current story is not a good testimony. We haven't demonstrated Jesus' love. Many of us have been internally focused. We even have shot our wounded. All this, as the world watched.

- Instead of being messengers with great Good News, we have presented bad news.

- Instead of loving our neighbors and our enemies, we've spoken about Jesus, but we've left people in need.

- Instead of loving each other and visibly living out Jesus' love and truth, we've fought with each other and fixated on inconsequential differences.

- Instead of unity and love, we've shown disunity and strife.

This must greatly grieve the heart of God. As a result of our behavior people don't want to hear:

- from us about Jesus;

- our words; or

- the Christian version of God.

Yet these same people still need the Good News. They simply don't know they have this need. When the economy was good and life seemed manageable, people embraced hope. The fact that things are getting worse is actually great news for Good News people. It's often when people are faced with bad news, that they're desperate to hear some good news—any kind of good news. We have the greatest Good News.

God is opening a door for us to again step into our calling to live as agents of reconciliation.

For us to live as his sent ones, it's essential to love God. If we love God, honestly, and genuinely, his Spirit will help us to live in unity as churches—as the Church. We can recommit to being the people Jesus prayed we'd be before he left earth.

We need to love each other. If we keep our eyes on Jesus, then loving each other, warts and all, is a lot easier. We do not necessarily need to like each other. We need to love each other. This love is an action rather than a feeling. In the West, love is associated with feeling, therefore, we think we need to like each other. If we do not like each other than we think we do not love each other. We do not need to have warm fuzzy's for each other. Jesus says we have to love each other. I think it means we need to love Jesus enough so we put up with the sharp edges, wrinkles, and warts of our brothers and sisters. It means hard work, but if we fail to love each other, the world will never know we serve a God who loves us and them…he loves us, in spite of all our sharp edges, wrinkles, and warts. We need to love them with the love of Jesus, and the key is to do this in unity as the Church.

As the World Watches

Intentionally loving together as the Church is the big, new challenge. It's imperative to learn to live and love in such a way that we show a united front to a watching world. People in the world are watching. We can only share the needed Good News when we present the united front that represents our true reality as Jesus' people.

We'll have an impact as agents of reconciliation when we actually look like we share the same love, the same message, and we're on the same page.

We can only bring reconciliation when we love each other and look like we love each other. People can only hear the Good News when we demonstrate love in action. We don't have to say words. Words alone are not enough. Too many words have been spoken already. The most important thing we as God's people can do is to tell Jesus' story in action.

In his first letter, the Apostle Peter instructs us to be ready to give an answer to anyone who asks us to give a reason for the hope we have.[4] We aren't told to go tell everyone about Jesus and to get them to pray "the prayer." If we read Peter's words carefully, we realize it includes the assumption people notice our hope, and they will ask us about it.

People will only ask us questions if:

- ☙ they see something that stands out—if we live in a way they do not expect.

- ☙ we live in such a way they wonder what makes us different.

Let's live in a way that positively and counterculturally stands out.

We Tell "Our" Gospel

Currently among churches and Christians, there's much emphasis on social justice. It flows out of churches embracing a social gospel; the application of Christian principles to social problems.[5] Doing good and embracing social justice issues carries a risk for the Church. When we focus on fixing the social problems, it can hinder us from following Jesus' leading and cause us to emphasize social justice—doing good for the sake of doing good. Social justice cannot be the end goal for the Church. As Christians, it's of paramount importance to provide practical help to people in need! No question. We serve a God who has great love for and concern for the poor and needy. As his children, our love needs to be the same—to actively demonstrate concern and provide care for the poor, needy, disadvantaged, and oppressed.

But let's remember, our greatest need in the world is not fixing the social, physical, emotional or economic ills. The greatest need is for people to come to know Jesus and to be reconciled to God. Meeting needs and serving people in the community can be a great tool to demonstrate the love of Jesus, as long as it does not become an end in itself and replacing the Gospel.

The dilemma of balancing the meeting of needs and preaching the true Gospel has faced the Church over the ages. We don't want to use people's needs to force the Gospel on them. At the same time, we don't want to become focused only on people's needs.

Jesus calls us to love people and care for their needs without strings attached. As we live a life of love toward God and toward others, we will naturally care for the needs of people around us. If we lived a life of love to our neighbors, wouldn't they want to know more about the one who is our Lord?

God chose people to demonstrate his love and power to people in our communities as individuals. But we're also chosen to demonstrate his love as organizations.

It's important, as local churches and Christian organizations, to demonstrate God's love together. If we do good as individuals, or even as an isolated local church or nonprofit, people might think we're great people. Only when people see us doing good *together* will they be able to see Jesus. He chose the Church to live out his life in the community in such a way that people take notice and desire more of God and of his love. When they see more than a "good person" or a "good organization" they might begin to understand and want more of his love, more of him. When love is lived out, people can see and think, "I want more of that!" People will come based on their physical and emotional needs. When they do it presents open doors for God's love to be poured out. As we meet people's needs we always need to keep in mind that our true mandate is to be agents of reconciliation—not just aid providers.

People's greatest need is for God and a relationship with him. If the only Gospel we preach and live out is the social gospel, how does that ultimately help anyone? If we feed them today, they will be hungry again tomorrow. If we bind up their wounds today, they will still be hurting tomorrow. Caring for needs alone is not enough.

As churches we cannot transition from living as a social club
into working as a social service agency!

It's essential to the work of the Kingdom to love people and care for them in Jesus' name. Without love in his name, it's a pointless exercise. They'll still be in need on earth, and we may hinder many from enjoying eternity in God's presence. We can never forget to love people with the love that God has for them. As we care for them, our longing should be that they receive all God has for them, which is reconciliation to him through a saving relationship with Jesus Christ.

The Church can no longer just speak words because words alone leave people physically hungry and empty. However, we also can't merely live out a social gospel because simply alleviating needs leaves people spiritually hungry and empty.

As God's people, it's our mandate to:
- ເ៩ know and live out God's truth;

- ເ៩ live as lovers of people and lovers of God; and

- ເ៩ live our faith in action without diluting the truth of the Gospel.

This leads me to ask:
- ເ៩ How do we practically demonstrate God's love in order to meaningfully preach the truth of Jesus through our actions?

- ເ៩ What does it mean to truthfully live our faith in action?

- ເ៩ How do we bring the real Good News in a way that can be received and heard?

In Chapter 5, *Demonstrate His Love In Community*, we discussed how as individuals, we can bring this ministry of reconciliation. It's through missional volunteering and connecting. As individuals, intentionally living missionally and incarnationally, is one great way to "preach" the Good News. Does it stop there? Is that the only place for this kind of cooperation and collaboration with God to bring reconciliation to the world?

The ministry of reconciliation has been co-opted and hamstrung because we haven't taken it far enough. We have conveniently identified the local church as the hope of the world. The local church isn't the hope of the world. Jesus is the hope of the world! The local church is the vehicle for that hope. And, local churches need to partner with his Church for this hope to be noticed and experienced in the world.

The local church plays a key role. Jesus' chosen instrument to bring hope to the world is his Church. We gather in local communities—little "c" churches (regardless of size)—together making up *the* Church, his Church. Jesus didn't intend for each local expression of his Church, his body, to be independent operators.

We Are the Church When We Partner

When we think the local church is the hope of the world, we start behaving as if bringing hope to the world depends on us—as specific local churches. Each church does not need to do everything there is to do in a community to demonstrate Jesus' love. When we try to do it all, it spells t-r-o-u-b-l-e for everyone. One consequence is that the watching world around us sees churches competing instead of loving. As local churches, we become more internally focussed and protective when we live as if our local church expression is the entire body. When we live internally focussed, we no longer exhibit the love and life of Jesus to a watching world that needs Good News. Each local church has a role in the overall Church. It's when we partner, we are the Church.

The body of Christ and partnering as organizations can also include those nonprofit organizations that live out Jesus' mission in the world. Many of these were started because local churches could not or would not be the hands and feet of Jesus in the community. People called to love people in the community with the love of Christ had no choice but to answer that call outside the walls of the local church. So often local churches communicate that ministry is serving at the church or in church approved opportunities. Anyone called beyond that finds no place to serve. Pastors lament that only twenty percent of people do eighty percent of the work. Maybe twenty percent of the people should do eighty percent of the work! What if God designed the other eighty percent to serve in the community?!

Jesus tells us where two or three are gathered in his name, he is in their midst.[6] We, his people, are the church when we gather—whether that is in a traditional setting, house church, missional community, small group or volunteer community.

Whatever way we choose to gather as God's people, we need to remember we are his Church. We need to work together with other organizations. Together, we need to demonstrate and live out the life of Jesus today.

In much of the Western Hemisphere, fewer and fewer people attend church. Even regular attendees come less frequently. Regular attendance used to mean weekly, now it often means semi-monthly and monthly. Many people never attend church. Only a small percentage of people are really connected in their church community and embrace a genuine relationship with Jesus. This means most people are not attending, and they do not have this relationship with Jesus. So our programs, advertising and attractional activities all compete for a shrinking "market." Most of us are not structured to reach those who do not yet have a vibrant relationship with Jesus. What's up with that?

If we were businesses, we would compete for market share and try to expand the market. We wouldn't all try to go after the same few customers. And yet, the church with the greatest message of all time, generally limits itself to the few, and tends to forget about the rest. This cannot be what Jesus had in mind when he said, "By this all men will know that you are my disciples." The point is to reach those beyond the walls who do not yet know him. So how do we reach them with the love of Jesus? How did Jesus reach people?

In our typical church paradigm, God the Father would have sent Jesus out as a church planter into this foreign land, Samaria. He would have started a missional synagogue. He would have had a great program. He would have had the missional synagogue open 24 hours a day, and sat in its midst. People could have come in any time and talked to him, ask questions or get help. That is what we typically do as churches.

That isn't what Jesus did. He went to various places, and he loved the people he found there. A lot of these people were disconnected from God. From our perspective, he did the weird stuff. He sat on the well to meet the woman who approached, carrying her water bucket. He came to where he knew she would come. She could not ignore him. He loved her. He treated her—not like a typical Jewish rabbi—but like the Messiah who wanted her to be reconciled with the God who created her. What if we:

- take Jesus' approach?
- collaborate and meet people where they live?
- collaborate and address their hurts and needs?
- combine our efforts as churches to love our communities?

It's Time to Rethink Our Approach

We as the Church need to rethink our approach. We need to collaborate and cooperate. It is going to take all of us to demonstrate Jesus' love to a watching and dying world!

Reaching the poor, needy, and disadvantaged requires the whole Church. Together, we can:

- provide real answers to the social, economic, physical, and emotional needs while growing God's Kingdom for his glory.
- do good and reach people with the love of Jesus.
- change the tide and reverse the trend.
- spread the Good News and win people to Jesus.
- bring the ministry of reconciliation.

It's important to partner to reach those in need with the love of Jesus. One essential difference is to go beyond just plugging in our own people. It'll work if we do it together. Let's collaborate. Let's encourage organizations, of all kinds, to partner with other organizations of all kinds: churches with churches, nonprofits with nonprofits, churches and nonprofits together. Let's be the Church together.

One of my pet peeves is doing something already being done well by someone else. Why does it bother me? Well, my question is, "Why spend good money to do what is already being done?" Why create new administration with the necessary overhead and spend good money to do the same thing another community organization is doing except with a flavor difference? Why do this instead of partnering? Certainly there's enough to do and enough people to reach for everyone of us to play a role. We, as churches, have often operated with a scarcity mentality, as if there are just a few lost people, and we need to rush to get there first or do it the best. Jesus told his disciples that the harvest is plentiful, but the workers are few.[7] There is not too small of a harvest. No. There are too few workers.

One area where we see this concept at work is in great disasters, such as the January 2010 earthquake in Haiti. Understandably, organizations rush to help, but there is often such a duplication of effort. Most of those helping are also reaching out for donations. Of course, we need to help, but I believe we can find a better way. What if we partnered, communicated, decided, and worked together to tackle the big project? Instead of all fighting for the same dollars, personnel, or turf, we could partner and accomplish more together.

Unfortunately, this doesn't only happen during massive natural disasters. We even do this at the local level in churches and nonprofits. My friend, Ed, tells me that the number two rule in fundraising is, "Everyone gives to an emergency." People, organizations, businesses, and celebrities all hold fundraisers and drives during a disaster or crisis. Much money, even with the bleak economic conditions, comes in to help during great natural disasters. The fact that people want to help is great, but how are we ensuring that the maximum good will be done after a crisis? How will the money be spent? Maybe the crisis prompts everyone to jump in, but should this be our motivation as Christians and churches? What good works will not continue because the money was re-directed to disaster relief? Many organizations want to do good, but without collaboration their efforts will not reach their full potential.

Is there any hope? The Christian community seems more inclined to collaborate now than it has for many years, decades, and maybe even centuries. God continues to bring a desire to live missionally and be collaborative to many different people and organizations. The tide is changing and people are seeking to work together.

It's Time to Collaborate

Why should we collaborate? Obviously one of the key reasons is to reach people disconnected from God with the love of Christ. It requires all of us and the many different expressions of the body of Christ to effectively reach the community with the love of Jesus. Nobody and no organization can do all things for all people. Not only is it impossible, it is also not part of God's plan. Jesus intends for each one of us to give and live in the way he created us. We each have an aspect of his character and gifts that need to be shared in the context he placed us. Local churches and local organizations also have a grouping of gifts, skills, and resources Jesus intends for them to share in the community, at the time, and within the context he determined. We all bring much needed aspects that can reach a watching and needy world.

Just like the body metaphor as employed by the Apostle Paul[8] describes the unique functions of individual members, it also describes the greater workings of the Church at large. The purpose is to be one Church and to grow as each body part does its work. Each local church is a part of the body and has a unique function. No church can say to another church they are not needed. No local church is supposed to fulfill all the roles and play all the functions. Each church has a unique calling and assignment from God as part of his plan to expand his Kingdom. Each church is to do its part, but all parts are needed. The separate local churches, as separate body parts, do not need to compete with each other or try to do each other's jobs. The hand should not say to the foot that it can stay home because the hand will do the footwork as well. Neither should the foot compete with the hand to be more important or powerful. The hand should do the work of the hand. The foot should do the work of the foot. Each part should do its God-given task. God is the one who gifts people and local expressions of his body for the tasks he has determined they should do. God assigns the tasks. God sets how much reach and influence each person and each church has; it's according to his plan. Let's not look to each other and compete.

Another reason to collaborate is to present a cohesive story. How will people understand God and the love of God if we do not tell it? The only way it can really be heard and understood is if it is told in a cohesive way. The story needs to be a cohesive story. They can only hear the story if we tell it in a compelling way. It is only compelling if we live lives that make sense to them. They need to see it lived out.

The best way to tell it is when we collaborate. The world needs to see and experience the truth of Jesus and the truth of his love. This story needs to be told and it needs to be told by the Church—together. The unity of our witness is the convincing factor. What if we worked together? What if we combined our efforts to tell the story?

> *I am convinced many churches forego their best contribution*
> *to people's lives and to the community by trying to be everything*
> *(or by trying to be someone else's idea*
> *of church for them) rather than being who God made them to be.*
>
> —Reggie McNeal

Let's Collaborate for Community

When we collaborate we can create solutions rather than treat symptoms. In a nearby local city, there are a minimum of five organizations giving out food—some are food banks, others are churches with food donation ministries. Each organization collects and distributes food to local families. What they do is great and necessary but in the end, all they do is serve meals for that day. These food banks go to the same sources to get their food and supplies. They compete for the same resources: food, volunteers and donations. What if they combined their efforts? What if they had a more intentional plan to reach people? Could they reach more people working together? Could they address the issue of hunger rather than merely stocking shelves and providing much needed meals?

Through collaboration, we would be solving problems instead of dolling out bandaids. As churches and Christians we need to collaborate for community. The world around us longs for relationship, love and community. The communities around us need Jesus and he has sent us into the community to spread his love. To fulfill his commandments we need to collaborate. Rather than living separately and attempting to fulfill his commission and commandments in isolation, we need to collaborate so we can do more good—together.

We need to find ways to be the Church together—as churches, Christians and nonprofits. We need to see the Christian community united to positively affect people in our neighborhoods. By collaborating for community, we could solve problems and come up with real solutions. We could work together and plan for real change. When we collaborate as organizations, we can embrace and deploy each of our unique contributions. One church, as part of the community solution, could be recognized as more of a "foot church" and be known and celebrated for doing the foot stuff really well. A local nonprofit might be celebrated as an exemplary "hand" and contribute the hand part of the community better than others. These organizations then could partner with another church just down the block that is more of a "heart church." One does the foot stuff really well, another does the hand stuff better, and a third brings the heart to the community. If we map our separate contributions within the community and then choose for effective collaboration seeing each other as partners to reach the world with the love of Jesus, we can do more good—together. As part of community collaboration, we can choose not to be afraid to lose "our" people. Of course they are not really our people…they are God's people. So, we do not have to be afraid to lose them because we all belong to God, and we are all committed to reach the community together.

Make This Dream a Reality

When we think about it, collaboration shouldn't be difficult.

As churches, what if:

- all the pastors in a city, community, or region gather to pray for their communities?

- churches and pastors share their visions and intentionally collaborate to reach the community?

- we practice an abundance mentality and ask the Lord of the harvest to send workers and reap the harvest?

- we each do what we are uniquely assigned to do and trust God to assign someone else the rest?

- we genuinely love our people and help them find the best fit—even if that is at another local church?

- we trust God to bring us the people he has for us?

- we focus on the mission and the Kingdom rather than on numbers?

- we trust God to do more with our talents and gifts than we can do ourselves?

- we partner in local communities and actively demonstrate God's love through active involvement?

As nonprofits, what if:

- all executive directors connect and intentionally collaborate to serve the community better?

- we share our visions and collaborate for greater impact?

- we practice an abundance mentality and ask the Lord of the harvest to provide donations and volunteers?

- we each do what we are uniquely assigned to do and trust God to assign someone else the rest?

- we genuinely love the people we want to help and refer them to the best organization for their situation—even if that is another local nonprofit?

- we trust God to bring us the clients and resources he has for us?

- we focus on God's mission rather than our personal mandates?

- we trust God to give us greater success than we can accomplish ourselves?

One way to partner and collaborate in community would be to get into networks and intentionally share the work. Instead of duplicating efforts, and each local organization doing the same thing with a slightly different twist, we could partner and expand the work. If the other church has a ministry to homeless people in the community, why start your own? If the other nonprofit down the street provides a great ministry to at-risk-youth, why try to do the same thing? Why not partner with them? If you have a ministry to the poor and disadvantaged, why not think broader and work with other churches and nonprofits? Why not invite them to participate? Why do we all have to duplicate efforts and replicate each other's ministries and services? Why not send your people with a passion for reaching the homeless to work with the church who has that ministry or focus? Or, why not send the volunteers passionate for at-risk-youth to work with the nonprofit working with teens? They can still worship at your church, participate in your groups, and do life with your community. They can still support your nonprofit. Or, maybe, they should attend the other church or go to the other organization down the street. We are all part of Jesus' body—he has enough harvest and resources for all of us.

Jesus sent us to demonstrate his love in action. Let's be willing to share and collaborate. We can be generous with each other and not give into operating from a scarcity mentality—even if donations are down and costs are up. After all, God owns the cattle on a thousand hills.[9] Jesus never modeled a scarcity mentality. He took a mere five loaves and two fish to feed 5000.[10] If he could do that then, can he not now provide for his Church and his work through the Holy Spirit? Can he not through us, combined, accomplish more than we can ask or imagine according to the power that is at work within us?[11] According to the Apostle Paul, we cannot even imagine all that God is able to do in and through us. He can do immeasurably more than our greatest imagination or request! Is that not a mind-blowing thought?!

* Why not join forces and do more of it together?

* Why not have the Lord of the universe do more through us together?

If we partner, we can deliver exponential impact instead of merely addition impact. Right now, as we work in the same community without intentionally partnering with each other, we have addition impact—at best. It might actually have a negative effect because the watching world doesn't understand why Christians, churches, and nonprofits who believe in the same God do not cooperate in the work. I believe we could have exponential impact through collaboration. Right now, we are only one church next to another church next to a nonprofit. In this model, one plus one plus one is only three. If we combine forces, we may have an exponential impact in the Kingdom of God and in our communities. We could reach so far beyond what we can do now.

God will do more through us when we do it together. He desires unity, and he has sent his Spirit into our hearts to unite us. When we participate together, we're truly Jesus' body. A cohesive body functions much better than disconnected body parts do on their own!

Can you imagine the shock throughout the world around us if we actually started living this way? People might be added daily to those being saved! People would want to know more. "There is something about you guys. What is it? What happened to you people? You suddenly seem to get along!"

Doing good together is doing more good! Together, we can reach further and accomplish more. Most churches desire to impact their community and to transform it with the love of Jesus. Most Christian nonprofits want to live out the compassion of Jesus.

How much more effective will this be if we do it together? When each organization does it part, the following happens:

- God is pleased.
- Jesus is glorified.
- People are able to see God's love in action.

Collaboration takes our egos out of the equation. It will finally be about Jesus, and he would be delighted. He would receive all of the glory if it was about him, and we were less visible. I think Jesus would honor our efforts if we made it about him. We might even grow bigger churches, nonprofits, and ministries because it would not be about our success but Jesus' name.

Living It Out

Let's dream about the possibility of seeing a community of believers united to impact their local community. Imagine the impact! Can you sense God's pleasure? How good and pleasant it is when people live and work in unity. Jesus prayed for this before he suffered and died. He commanded us to live a life of love to demonstrate his love. He came to reconcile us to God and to each other. We are designed for unity in community. Let's live out our wiring and purpose to demonstrate Jesus' love to a watching world! Let's be the Church and, together, expand God's Kingdom and spread the Good News to his glory!

Key Concepts

- When we partner as Christians, churches, and nonprofits, we can do more good together.
- Jesus' goal for his Church is to live, love, worship, and witness in unity.
- When a community of believers lives in unity, it demonstrates the truth of the Gospel.
- We are sent as agents of reconciliation. As we live in harmony, love God, love each other, and love our neighbor, the world will see, hear, and experience that Jesus is still the Savior of the world.

- We need to bring the Good News to a watching world through love lived out. It will require the whole Church demonstrating love in action.

- Churches and nonprofits need to collaborate to reach lost people with the love of Christ and to tell a cohesive story of God's love.

- When we partner, we can have greater impact on our community—providing solutions rather than bandages.

- By collaborating in community, we can be used by God to grow his Kingdom for his glory.

Questions for Living It Out

1. How can you collaborate to demonstrate Jesus' love to the community?

2. How are you practicing living in unity with churches and organizations in your context?

3. How do you practically demonstrate God's love so the truth of Jesus is preached meaningfully through your actions?

4. What does it mean for your organization to truthfully live your faith in action in partnership with others?

5. How do you bring the real Good News in a way that can be received and heard? Are you partnering with others to accomplish this?

6. How are you practicing an abundance mentality and asking the Lord of the harvest for the workers and resources?

7. Are you committed to focussing on what you were uniquely assigned to do and trust God to assign someone else the rest?

8. Do you believe there is enough for all of us?

Notes

1. See Ephesians 2:14

2. See John 17:3

3. Ephesians 4:1-5, CEV

4. See 1 Peter 3:15

5. A movement started in the late nineteenth century.

6. See Matthew 18:20

7. See Matthew 9:37

8. See 1 Corinthians 12:12-31

9. See Psalm 50:10

10. See Mark 6:30-44

11. See Ephesians 3:19-21

Chapter 9

Let Your Story Lead

*The revolution starts with you, doing what you are capable of doing,
regardless of what others are doing. Leadership is not about being or doing what
is popular. It is about doing what is right, simply because it is right…
You, personally, are responsible for revolutionizing the world.
You cannot do it alone, but it cannot be done without you.*

—George Barna

*Leadership development comes through character development,
because leadership is a character issue. Therefore, the first truth in leadership
development is this: God's assignments are always based on character—
the greater the character, the greater the assignment.*

—Henry Blackaby

Rita's Story

For over twenty years, my friend, Rita, led a local missional nonprofit in Seattle. When she took the job, Rita believed her experience had prepared her to take on the challenge of leading this ministry to street kids. As a strong spiritual leader, she invested in leadership and in herself. Consequently, her skills and character grew as she built up the organization.

After a few years of hard work with some good success, exhaustion gripped her life. The organization needed more, and at night, she agonized whether or not she was the person for the job. Deeply searching her heart, she analyzed her work experience, her set of skills and her team, but nothing bubbled to the surface that shouted, "That's it! I'll change this, and everything will be fine!"

In her tiredness and despair, she cried out to God. "Lord, I've invested every bit of myself and then some to this job, and now I only feel exhausted and overwhelmed. Please help me. I can't do this without your help. I can't do this job alone, but I don't want to fail…not myself and not others."

Rita refused to go on without God's tangible and specific help. She prayed and remained in God's presence until he provided her with what was needed. God showed up powerfully, and he showed her the way…not a big blue print for success, but a process to lead the organization under his guiding hand. Rita learned to lead counterculturally and counterintuitively to typical leadership approaches. Rita became a missionally-minded spiritual leader.

As a result of her encounter with God, she devoted long periods of time in the Word and in prayer. Her commitment was to lead the organization and her teams based on her relationship with Jesus—rather than primarily focusing on leadership principles. She grew in her knowledge and relationship with God. She would listen to God to hear his direction for the organization, and then she'd carry out her responsibilities based on his leading. She learned principles of leadership from studying Scripture and observing Jesus' ways with his disciples and other people he encountered.

She spent intentional and significant time with Jesus. Her leadership teams benefited from what she had heard, learned, or discerned in her time with him. She also taught her teams how to spend time with Jesus and listen to his leading.

She would include time in team meetings for listening to Jesus together. She trusted he would lead and bring them to unity of vision and decision. She and her leaders were committed to hearing from God and not to move forward until they all agreed. They led out of unity. She took her leaders through a process of going deep with the triune God: Father, Son and Holy Spirit. Out of this process, she led the organization—together with her team.

Rita took the next steps in the ministry's development and growth as God opened doors and led her and her teams. She had an absolute rule: unless she had spent time with Jesus, heard from him, and he affirmed her decision, she would not move forward. She practiced sitting at his feet and would not move out of his presence until she knew what he wanted from her on any key issues and decisions.

The organization blossomed under her leadership. She raised millions of dollars for her nonprofit and the ministry to urban street kids. She did amazing work based on her relationship with Jesus.

Rita is a strong leader with keen vision, passion, and drive, yet she surrendered her natural abilities to Jesus and chose to follow him and his leading.

Rita led by:
- daring to take her people deeper into their relationship with God.
- leading missionally to reach homeless kids with the love of Jesus.
- pointing to Jesus and leaving a Kingdom impact on her employees, volunteers, and clients.

We Need Missional Leaders

Why a Chapter on Leadership?

Leading a missional revolution requires Christ-centered, Spirit-filled leadership. Every movement hinges on leadership. How much more important is great leadership in a movement to advance God's Kingdom? Passionate visionary leaders are necessary to lead the Church on a missional revolution—back into the streets, following in Jesus' footsteps.

Jesus brought the ultimate revolution: freeing people from a worldly, oppressive kingdom into God's glorious Kingdom. He organically approached the process. He lived out the truth and chose twelve unlikely men to be the leaders to advance his Kingdom. Maybe he chose these men because through them he would make it clear that the establishment of his rule came through his Spirit and power—not because of their personality and leadership skills.

> *Jesus was the consummate leader.*
> *No other person in history has been in*
> *higher demand than he was.*
>
> —Henry and Richard Blackaby

Jesus led the twelve and through them the Church—from the first century until today. He took his message to the people and into the streets. Jesus never hid in buildings or withdrew from the world. He lived, walked, and taught among the people. His disciples followed his leadership. He expects us to do the same. For those of us who have been called and gifted to lead, we need to follow Jesus out of our boxes and into the world…living, leading, and teaching among the people.

Advancing the Missional Revolution Requires a Great Leader

For many years, I thought of a leader as a charismatic person who commands everyone's attention. The kind of person who walks into a room and everyone notices. While this image describes some leaders, it does not fit all of us. I know I am not that type of leader. That used to be my picture of what leadership encompassed. I didn't fit the picture. Therefore, I didn't think of myself as a leader.

Sometimes God calls us to lead, but we don't respond because we don't believe we're leaders. We can feel unqualified because we don't have the right lens. Leaders come with various styles and personalities. God created each leader as an original. Over time, I discovered God called and gifted me to lead—in the way I am wired. I need to follow him and lead the way he designed me.

While not everyone is called to be a leader, those who are gifted, need to step up and lead. Especially for this missional revolution, advancing this movement requires strong leaders who may not fit the traditional leadership type. Godly leaders are called and gifted. If Jesus tapped you on the shoulder to lead, it's essential to do it well. The Apostle Paul tells us that if God has given us leadership ability, it's important to take the responsibility seriously and lead diligently.[1] The advancement of his Kingdom depends on leaders following Jesus and leading well.

It takes a leader to move the mission forward. I subscribe to the maxim, "You can't lead anyone else further than you have gone yourself."[2] This is true for all leaders, but it's especially essential for leaders in God's Kingdom.

As leaders, let's consider the following questions:

- Unless we have sat with Jesus and received from him, how do we guide others?

- Unless we have let God lead us into deep places, how can we lead others there?

Given the importance of the task, let's commit to leading well. Developing into the best possible leaders, requires us to:

- know God;

- spend time with God and listen to him, so we can lead others; and

- understand ourselves, know our call, and do our part.

The Bible tells us that not many of us should desire to be teachers because they will be held to a higher standard.[3] The same rule applies to leadership. Anyone who seriously and authentically follows Jesus, especially as a leader, knows it is very challenging to follow God into his work. True leadership is for those who are willing and prepared to lead in times of plenty and in times of need; and to lead in times of cooperation and in times of adversity. A true leader knows it's not a popularity contest, but rather it's staying true to doing God's will no matter what the personal cost.

Leaders carry more responsibility and have fewer privileges—at least, that's how it should be. True leaders work harder, sacrifice more, and go the extra mile. True spiritual leaders follow Jesus, the best leader that has ever lived and led. He chose followers, led them, taught them, delegated to them, and he eventually died for the "cause." In all he did, he looked to the Father and followed his will absolutely. A true spiritual leader lives to accomplish God's will.

As leaders in the missional revolution, we're stepping out to follow God into new territory to take back what the enemy has stolen. Leaders who follow Jesus face warfare. God equips those he calls for this battle, and he requires them to grow in character and in relationship with him. He will deepen us, heal us, stretch us, and challenge us to get more serious about him and about the work.

According to author and spiritual director, Ruth Haley Barton, when you are called to be a leader, you are first and foremost called to be yourself, the self God created you to be. It's important to be authentic and live out what we are supposed to do in his Kingdom. God makes no mistakes and knows who we are. He made us and created the tasks and context he called us into. Part of answering the call, is understanding ourselves, our wiring, and our leadership.

When God calls us to lead, he prepares our character and us. He provides assignments and gives us opportunities to grow—in our leadership and in our character. There will be challenges to stretch us. God prepares us for the work ahead of the work. Getting ready involves a process.

Propelling the Missional Revolution Requires a Spiritual Leader

Leadership is assuming the responsibility for going from where you are to where you need to go. It involves motivating people and creating change. Leadership is hard work. There usually is a lot at stake, and there's much involved to succeed. Yet, sometimes our involvement is only to obey God's leading, and others will take it to its successful conclusion. Some of us may be like Moses, and we'll never be able to enter the Promised Land, but we'll provide the leadership for those who will be able to cross the river.

While all leadership involves creating movement, Henry Blackaby contends spiritual leadership is about moving people onto God's agenda.[4] In his great book, *Spiritual Leadership*, he explains that not all Christian leaders are spiritual leaders. We are spiritual leaders only when we are moving people onto God's agenda. Spiritual leaders bring people from their own plan onto God's plan.

Spiritual leadership has more to do with who we are and our relationship with God than how we approach the tasks and work of leadership. Clearly the principles, practices, and tasks of leadership are important. We need to spend time leading people. They will not be moved onto God's agenda when we spend all our time alone with God. It requires a balance of time with God and doing the work of leading. Blackaby's definition of a spiritual leader expands our understanding of who and what a leader is. From this perspective, anyone who has an authentic relationship with God can be a leader because even if we move just one person onto God's agenda we are leading. In this sense, the number of followers doesn't define leadership.

Leadership includes an ingredient called "followership." With spiritual leadership, it's about moving people onto God's agenda—leading people to follow Jesus. The Apostle Paul talks about this kind of leading and following when he writes, "Follow my example, as I follow the example of Christ."[5] Spiritual leadership is less about being a dynamic, charismatic leader with many followers. It is about leading others as we follow Jesus' leadership.

Accepting the role of a spiritual leader is a Kingdom assignment initiated and led by God. We can't decide to move people onto God's agenda. We might have the desire and passion and make ourselves available, but we cannot say, "I am a spiritual leader." According to Blackaby, "Spiritual leadership is a noble undertaking, but it's something that God must assign."[6] We can ask God to make us spiritual leaders, but we can't make that happen. God knows his agenda for people and the world. It's his task to move people onto his agenda, and he invites those he chooses to partner with him to lead people. Spiritual leadership is like sharing the Gospel: it's our assignment to share the Good News, but we cannot cause people to believe. Only God can draw people and bring them to faith in him. It is similar to spiritual leadership, it's essential that we lead as God directs, but we cannot cause people to move onto God's agenda. That's God's job.

Spiritual leadership flows out of our relationship with God. If we desire to be spiritual leaders, then let's first focus on our relationship with God. It's about knowing and being known by him. When we talk about leading people onto God's agenda, it's essential to have spent enough time with him to know what his will and plans are. We need to hear from him what he desires to accomplish and, as part of this, what he has for us to do. Jesus spent time with his Father every day—early in the morning, late at night, sometimes throughout the night. He makes it clear that even though he is God, he did as his Father led him. He said it this way, "I tell you the truth, the Son can do nothing by himself; he can do only what he sees his Father doing, because whatever the Father does the Son also does."[7] Spiritual leaders follow Jesus' example because it is all about him.

Spending time with God is a spiritual leader's antidote to living too busy a life. God doesn't give us more to do than we can handle. We allow this scenario to happen to ourselves. There have been many times in my leadership, where I have taken on more than I can do. Most of these things were good things. At the time, I thought they were from God. During those times, when I took on too much, I always seemed to be running, teetering on the edge of anxiety, and overcome with stress.

One of those times when it was clear to me that I couldn't go on and something had to give, I asked God to help me understand why this happened repeatedly in my life. During my time with him, God reminded me that Jesus' yoke is easy and his burden light.[8] That's not what I had been experiencing—the tasks felt overwhelming and heavy. Either Jesus' words were untrue or I was seriously out of sync.

Since I believed Jesus' words are true, it led me to evaluate my approach and seek clear answers from God. It took time for me to see and understand the truth.

God showed me to avoid this dilemma requires:

- spending a significant amount of my time with him. Authentic time.

- intentionally and diligently seeking God and sitting at his feet, listening to his wisdom and guidance for my life.

When I genuinely seek to hear from God, and I understand what he is asking me to do, I've always found:

- God doesn't give me more to do than I can handle.

- when I spend deep and authentic time with God, I discover that Jesus' burden is easy and his yoke light.

- what he gives me to do is achievable in the time he has allowed.

- if my experience differs, then I probably have taken on more than he gave me to do or I've not spent enough or sincere time with him.

Time with him is critical because it's the only place where we can learn God's will and the plans he has for us. Sometimes we've traveled so far down the road of assigning stuff to ourselves, without checking with God, that our list of things becomes too great and the burden too heavy. As a result, we're confused and insecure in how to change the situation for the better.

God can bring order into the chaos. It probably will take some time to undo this list of "Too Much To Do," and to reduce the pile to the size

God has intended for us. When we come to the realization we're out of sync, it's best to make the commitment to get back to God's assignments.

It takes discipline to spend time with God. We can easily fall into the trap of getting so busy doing good things *for* God that we don't have time to be *with* God. Surprisingly, when we spend time with him, sometimes he leads us to do nothing, but be still and spend more time with him. It's counterintuitive for leaders to be inactive and still before God. Sometimes the very thing God tells us to do in preparation for what he has for us to accomplish is, "Be still. Spend time with me. Know that I am God."

As a leader, this is difficult to do because there is so much that needs to be done. However, if we're not going anywhere because God is not leading us there or the timing is not right, then all we're doing is running in place. We may even be going backward and losing ground! Sitting still would be more productive than endless busyness without purpose. This kind of busyness causes us to be out of breath and perspiring. We might feel good because we have been active, but in effect, we've gone nowhere and done nothing. In the process, we've expended unnecessary energy to get nowhere fast. The energy we wasted is the energy God might have wanted to preserve for the next leg of our assignment. How much better would it be to sit with God, hear from him, and follow his lead? If we simply rested, we would still be in the same spot as when we're running in place, but we would be energized and ready for his assignment.

Henry Blackaby puts it this way, "I think God is crying out and shouting to us, 'Don't just do something. Stand there! Enter into a love relationship with me. Get to know me. Adjust your life to me. Let me love you and reveal myself to you as I work through you.' A time will come when the doing will be called for, but we cannot skip the relationship. The relationship with God must come first."[9]

When we lead out of a deep relationship with God, we have the real assurance that whatever he is leading us to do is what he has in mind. He has gone ahead and prepared us and the work for us so we will be able to do what he intends. The authority we have to lead comes from having spent time with Jesus. When we lead out of our time with Jesus, that authority will flow out of us, and people will know. They will be following Jesus through us. This will cause his name to be glorified and his will to be done.

If Jesus could do nothing without his Father, how can we? He said it plainly, "I am the vine; you are the branches. If you remain in me and I in you, you will bear much fruit; apart from me you can do nothing."[10] Even as leaders we are just branches…without him we are dead wood.

We are qualified to lead when we have spent time in God's presence. Ruth Haley Barton writes of God's word to Moses, "The people will follow you because you have met me. Because you know my name deep in your being. That is what qualifies you to be a spiritual leader, and that's why people will be willing to follow you right from the place they have known for so long to a place that is brand new."[11] Our leadership success and effectiveness depends on time with God: Father, Son, and Holy Spirit.

Advancing the Missional Revolution Depends on a Missional Leader

Missional leadership differs from other leadership because of the context in which it takes place. The stakes of all leadership are high, but missional leaders exist to unleash people to be agents of reconciliation. The stakes are highest. If a missional leader fails, it affects people's eternal destiny. The missional leader's call is about nothing less than eternal life and death.

According to Alan Roxburgh, "A missional church is a community of God's people who live into the imagination that they are, by their very nature, God's missionary people living as a demonstration of what God plans to do in and for all of creation in Jesus Christ."[12] He adds, "God is about a big purpose in and for the whole creation. … Just as its Lord is a mission-shaped God, so the community of God's people exists, not for themselves but for the sake of the work. Mission is therefore not a program or project some people in the church do from time to time…the church's very nature is to be God's missionary people." The missional leader is the person who creates the culture and context allowing God's people to live missionally and incarnationally in the place and time of God's choosing, doing the good works that he prepared in advance for them to do.

Rita, as a missionally-minded executive director, created the right culture and context in her organization, and she led teams based on her relationship with Jesus. She spent time with him and then brought what he led her to do into her leadership. Her approach led her to have deep conversations with her followers and fellow leaders. She led by example. Through the practice of spending deeper times with Jesus as Christians and as leaders, she and her team led missionally—seeking God's guidance for the work.

Missional leadership facilitates the opportunities, community, and practice in order for God's people to discover their missionary calling and seek to learn and live out this calling in their daily lives. This kind of leadership is fluid, organic, and unpredictable. It requires a deep and strong relationship with God to lead God's people to become genuinely missional according to God's calling. It requires knowing what he has in mind for this community, at this time, and in this place. Missional leadership is exciting and dangerous. It occurs on the front lines.

Missional leaders and missional people live differently than other people. Reggie McNeal writes that missional people order their lives around a missionary purpose.[13] Missional leadership requires a different approach because the purpose is to reach lost people with the message of hope and invite them to a place where God can bring them back to him. Missional leaders lead their people to live lives that facilitate conversations. From there, they can bring people to a place where they can be reconciled to God.

Being missional is intentional and entrepreneurial. Missional leaders need to forge new methods because the new missional approach isn't what many churches have been doing for hundreds of years. Many Christians and leaders have lived in boxes and assumed people will come to us to find God. As missional leaders, it's key to follow the ultimate missional leader, Jesus. He sat on the well to reach the Samaritan woman and her village, not in a synagogue with an "open 24/7" sign. He followed his Father's lead, and he came to reconcile people to God. As he was sent, he sends us, the Church. The Church's greatest assignment is to share the Good News as agents of reconciliation.

Missional living requires intentionality. We cannot accidentally be on mission. We need missional leaders to create a movement of people who live purposely missional—to be agents of reconciliation and to reach lost people with the love of God.

As missional leaders, we need to help our people do serious missional good. Therefore, we need to be able to lead well. We need to do our part. We need to be leaders of integrity. We need to answer the calling to lead to the best of our ability—in our leading, in our attitude, and in our service. Let's strive to be spiritual leaders who lead missionally with focus and vision.

> Finally, the unmistakable mark of leaders who are authenticated by God is that they are like Christ. They function in a Christ like manner and those who follow them become more like Christ. ... A person is truly a spiritual leader when others are moved to be more like Christ.
>
> —Henry and Richard Blackaby

Leadership Ingredients for the Missional Revolution

Develop Self-Knowledge

As missional leaders, just like any great leaders, it's important to know ourselves. This includes understanding our wiring, passion, context, history, skills, gifts, and calling.

Understanding our past and present is essential to grow as excellent spiritual leaders. It's key to keep our focus on spiritual growth and emotional healing as they go hand-in-hand. These two aspects of our character are mutually limiting. We can strive to spiritually grow, but if we lack emotional health, it'll restrict how deep we can go with Jesus. When we heal emotionally, and all of us have emotional dents and dings, then we can spiritually grow on a deeper level. It works the other way too. As we go deeper with God, we increase our spiritual well-being, and we can develop the emotional courage and character to face the stuff we don't like about ourselves.

The more we are sure of God's love for us and knowing we're safe with him, the more we can grow and face those aspects of our character we don't like or are holding us back. Spiritual growth and emotional healing are important practices as part of equipping us to be the best leaders we can be.

As leaders let's learn and understand how God created us. Let's understand how we are wired.[14] Some great tools exist to help leaders know more about leadership strengths and personality preferences. Beyond knowing our natural abilities, discovering and developing our spiritual gifts provides us greater understanding of God's spiritual job description and equipping to answer his call on us.[15] Embracing our personality, strengths, and gifts should be very interesting for leaders who want to be all God has for them to be. Additionally our potential affect increases when, as leaders, we invest in our team, and know how each team member is wired. Understanding the strengths, personalities, and gifts of the entire team allows us to better deploy each person for maximum Kingdom effectiveness. There are great assessments available to discover a team's wiring. I prefer to use Gallup StrengthsFinder, Myers-Briggs Type Indicator, and spiritual gifts assessments.[16]

God created us and assigned the work he has for us to do. We are each unique and need to know our own original design in order to most effectively utilize it for God's Kingdom and purposes. As I like to say, "You are the only you we will ever have so be the best *you* you can be." It is incumbent upon all of us to be the best self—surrendered to God—we can be to answer God's call on our lives. Where are we called? Where are we supposed to serve? What is our context? Our call might be similar to the call of another leader, but in a different context and with different wiring. How each of us respond and lead might look completely different from one leader to the next.

Practice the Craft

Some people are born leaders, but most of us have to learn leadership as a craft. We learn the craft by understanding leadership and practicing the principles. We will not all be top-level leaders, but every one of us can improve our leadership skills and effectiveness. Improving our leadership quotient and character is important for all leaders, but it's especially important for missional leaders if we want to have an impact on the missional revolution. It's important for leadership to be based on inviolable core principles.

Let us:

- work on being the best leader we can be according to our wiring.

- understand leadership principles and exercise leadership skills and practices.

✿ keep studying and reading about leadership. (There are volumes written on leadership. Every leader needs to invest in learning about the craft of leadership.)

Grow in Integrity

As Christian missional leaders, one of our nonnegotiable principles should be integrity. I define integrity as thoroughly being who you are, doing what you say, and saying what you do. It entails being truthful, reliable, and genuine. Integrity depends on sound character, and it can only be sustained in communion with Jesus.

Jesus' life was the epitome of integrity. Even the Pharisees recognized that fact, "'Teacher,' they said, 'we know that you are a man of integrity and that you teach the way of God in accordance with the truth. You aren't swayed by men, because you pay no attention to who they are.'"[17]

> I define integrity as thoroughly being who you are, doing what you say, and saying what you do.

Integrity is essential for any leader who aspires to be like Jesus—exhibiting integrity of heart: a heart wholly devoted to God without falseness or falsehood.

Why do we need integrity? We need this attribute because God blesses those who live this way. "He holds victory in store for the upright, he is a shield to those whose walk is blameless."[18] All of us should choose to be leaders of integrity. Leading with integrity requires character. It also involves our attitude and the choices we make. Character is developed by daily choices and tested in trial. As the Apostle Paul writes, "…suffering produces endurance, and endurance produces character, and character produces hope, and hope does not put us to shame, because God's love has been poured into our hearts through the Holy Spirit who has been given to us."[19]

Integrity and character require emotional healing and spiritual growth. When we fail to deal with emotional issues and hurts, we endanger our leadership, our people, and ourselves. When we fail to invest in spiritual growth, we have no basis from which to lead people onto God's agenda.

In the Bible we read about many leaders but, shockingly, very few finished well. If we look at what tripped up people, it always involved character issues. As missional leaders, Jesus longs for us to choose to be leaders who lead well and finish well. To do so, it's important to be leaders of integrity and character.

One of the hardest things for leaders to do is lead ourselves. Therefore, it's critical to understand who we are and what we need as leaders. Being called to lead is a privilege not a right. In the United States, apparently more than six out of every ten Americans consider themselves to be leaders. The real number is much lower, according to Barna. He writes, "For what it's worth, our extensive research regarding a full range of factors related to leadership suggests that perhaps one out of every seven Americans is a leader."[20]

We're missional and spiritual leaders if God calls us. As his leaders, God calls us for his purposes to lead at his pleasure for his glory.

Missional leadership requires us to keep:
- spending time with God;
- taking time to heal;
- taking time to grow in the Lord's wisdom;
- learning about leadership; and
- applying leadership principles and practices.

Take Responsibility Seriously

When God calls a leader, it involves responsibility. It's the kind of responsibility that accepts and honors what's been entrusted to the leader. As leaders, we are expected to carry out what God has assigned to us. If we want to be great leaders, it's imperative to take responsibility for our actions, our decisions, and for our teams. We will only be credible when we do what we say we will do and live authentically. People trust leaders who are credible and responsible.

The Apostle Peter writes to the leaders and pastors of churches to be, "Shepherds of God's flock that is under your care, watching over them— not because you must, but because you are willing, as God wants you to be; not pursuing dishonest gain, but eager to serve; not lording it over those entrusted to you, but being examples to the flock."[21] When God calls us to lead, he expects us to care for the people he has entrusted to us. God expects us to serve as Jesus served and lead as he led. Let's follow in his footsteps and be leaders after God's heart. When we lead according to God's design, we will not only move the mission forward, but we will be examples to others who seek to lead.

Following Jesus' leadership means leaving the outcome of our work to him. The outcome in any given situation is not about us, up to us, or our responsibility. The outcome, when we follow Jesus' leadership, is his responsibility. When you do what God asks you to do, it doesn't guarantee a certain outcome. We tend to think, *if I do this (the thing God is asking me to do), God will bring about the outcome I expect.* But he doesn't promise that result. God's leading and our following doesn't necessarily relate to a certain outcome, although we often think it will or should. We might feel that if we do our part, then God will do his, and we'll achieve the expected results. Not necessarily. We still have to do our part, but it doesn't guarantee the outcome. We have to be obedient for the sake of obedience not based on outcome. It's important to lead out of obedience to Jesus. This can be hard for us. We tend to assume a certain outcome when we follow God's leading. If it doesn't happen, we might feel upset or let down by God. As leaders, it's our role to follow Jesus, our leader, and do what we have been told to do—regardless of the outcome. Whatever God's plans are depend on him and are his responsibility. Completing the tasks he gave us to do is our responsibility. It's essential to follow because he leads us.

Let Your Story Lead

Only leaders can teach, mentor, and bring up other leaders. It takes a leader to make a leader. When Jesus told his disciples to make disciples and teach them everything he taught them, he modeled leader multiplication. Jesus told his disciples to make disciples as they moved along in their lives and ministry. While they were going about their daily lives, they needed to make disciples wherever they went. As leaders, let's make disciples as we are "going" out of the outflow of our daily lives.

To make the kind of disciples Jesus mentioned, those who obey his teachings, requires us to be spiritual leaders who obey Jesus' teachings. Missional leaders need to intentionally make missional leader disciples. It will take many missional leaders who love Jesus to lead the missional revolution. The Apostle Peter writes to us as Christians, "Honor Christ and let him be the Lord of your life. Always be ready to give an answer when someone asks you about your hope."[22]

Let's lead in such a way that people ask us about our hope. We need to sprinkle our life and leadership with conversations that demonstrate how Jesus is a normal part of our everyday life. As leaders, it's our role to love people—other leaders, our followers, and those we seek to reach. Love is necessary for leaders because Jesus modeled it and commanded his followers to live a life of love. He told his twelve disciples, leaders of his missional movement, to "Love each other. Just as I have loved you, you should love each other. Your love for one another will prove to the world that you are my disciples."[23]

To disciple other leaders, it's important to get to know them—it's important to get to know how they are doing in their spiritual lives. We need to spend time with those we are mentoring and ask them the deep questions. Let's also learn how they're wired. If we don't know their personality, interests, and strengths, we can't fully develop them. It's up to us, as leaders, to deploy those who we are discipling according to their wiring.

It's important to:
- know those we are discipling;
- release them into their calling;
- mentor them;
- give them responsibility;
- delegate; and
- allow them to lead when ready.

Investing in and knowing our people is important because as leaders we are the only ones who can develop other leaders. It's essential to develop leaders to share the passion and the work. Let's invest in younger leaders. To bring up the next generation of leaders and to accomplish more, it's key to become great delegators. For effective delegation, let's develop or tap into systems of accountability while allowing people to do their part. One way to effectively release the next generation of leaders is through apprenticing. In an apprenticing model, we can use our best leaders to train the next group of leaders, investing in them in order to make more leaders who love and serve Jesus.

> *The truth is, God is on mission to redeem humanity. He is the only one who knows how to do it. Leaders must understand, as Christ did, that their role is to seek the Father's will and to adjust their lives to him.*
>
> —Henry and Richard Blackaby

Finish Well

As leaders, let's commit to leading well and to finishing well. Dr. Bobby Clinton, author of *The Mentor Handbook*, writes that of all the leaders in the Bible, few finished well.[24] Most of us want to leave a legacy and make a difference. The only way to do that is to live and lead with integrity in order to know we fought the good fight and finished the race in a way that brings honor and glory to God.

According to Bobby Clinton, leaders need to know themselves to finish well. Let's make the choice to live right. Most of us who lead will go through tough times, be misunderstood or mistreated, and face trials. During those times, the way we behave and the road we choose will affect our legacy. It's during the tough times, that we'll need to choose integrity. That is when we decide whether we are going to be a leader of character. When we choose to do the right thing, especially in tough times, our credibility and leadership equity will increase. People watch us at all times. When we handle the hard times with integrity and character, people see we are authentic, and it increases trust and loyalty. Over time, as we choose to do the right thing, people will notice. We will be known as leaders of integrity who can be trusted. Our integrity and character will be tested. All serious Christian leaders know that true faith and following Jesus is hard. It requires courage and character. Barna writes, "Jesus told us that it is not by your words that you will be known, but by your actions—the fruit of who you are and what you believe. What you produce for the Kingdom of God is your purpose and your legacy."[25]

Let's lead well because the Lord of the harvest has called us. As we discussed, the harvest is plentiful but the workers are few. Jesus tells us that there are not enough workers, and there are not enough leaders, especially spiritually sound, missional leaders.

It's important to raise up leaders who can lead missionally for missional effect—leaders with a different focus. Leading missionally is about growing, giving, and gaining for the Kingdom. It's not about going on a mission trip, but it's about living a missional lifestyle.

God is up to something big. His purpose from the beginning was to redeem people and reconcile them back to himself. God is a God of mission and on mission. His mission is to find his lost people and return them to a relationship with him. Jesus was sent by the Father to seek and save those who were lost. He created the Church to be God's missional workforce. As the Church, we are both on mission and the earthly foretaste of the Kingdom of God. We are like a rough draft of the perfect Kingdom to come. As the Church, we exist for the sake of the work. It's important to lead in such a way that we facilitate the opportunity for people to get back into a relationship with God.

Living It Out

As leaders, it's our role to get equipped for the missional work. It's our role to live missionally intentionally in our own life first. It's our role to do our part, get ready, and get on with the work. There is a world that needs to know Jesus. It's critical for leaders to set the example, live missionally, and lead missionally. Jesus didn't choose the Sadducees or Pharisees. He chose ordinary people and changed the world. The Lord of the Church is still looking for willing people who will follow him to reach people with his love. Are we ready to missionally and authentically answer the call to lead?

Key Concepts

    ✎ Everything depends on leadership. It takes a leader to move the mission forward.

    ✎ The missional revolution will require spiritual leaders who lead missionally.

- Missional leaders need to unleash people to live missionally and intentionally as agents of reconciliation.

- Leaders need to develop their self-knowledge, learn the craft, and keep learning about leadership.

- Leaders take the responsibility to lead seriously.

- Leaders need to live their stories and disciple other leaders.

- Leaders need to choose integrity and grow their character to finish well.

- Missional leaders need to spend time with Jesus and lead out of their relationship with him. Missional leaders get their authority from having been with Jesus.

Questions for Living It Out

1. Did God call you to lead? Do you have the gift of leadership?

2. Do you know your leadership wiring? Do you know how you are wired to excel?

3. Are you a Christian leader or a spiritual leader? How do you know?

4. Do you spend intentional time with Jesus so you can lead and guide others?

5. Has God led you into deep places? Are you leading others to go deep with God and Jesus?

6. Do you believe you can do nothing without Jesus?

7. Where are you called? Who and where are you supposed to serve? What is your context?

8. How does God want to deploy you to further the missional revolution?

Notes

1. See Romans 12:8

2. Gene Mauch, Major League Baseball player and manager

3. See James 3:1

4. Henry T. Blackaby and Richard Blackaby, *Spiritual Leadership: Moving People on to God's Agenda* (Nashville: Broadman & Holman Publishers, 2001), 20.

5. 1 Corinthians 11:1, NIV

6. Henry T. Blackaby and Richard Blackaby, *Spiritual Leadership: Moving People on to God's Agenda* (Nashville: Broadman & Holman Publishers, 2001), 285.

7. John 5:19, NIV

8. See Matthew 11:30

9. Henry T. Blackaby and Claude V. King, *Experiencing God: How to Live the Full Adventure of Knowing and Doing the Will of God* (Nashville: Broadman & Holman Publishers, 1994), 19.

10. John 15:5, NIV

11. Ruth Haley Barton, *Strengthening the Soul of Your Leadership: Seeking God in the Crucible of Ministry* (Downers Grove, IL: InterVarsity Press, 2008), 81.

12. Alan J. Roxburgh and Fred Romanuk, *The Missional Leader: Equipping Your Church to Reach a Changing World* (San Francisco: Jossey-Bass, 2006), xv.

13. Reggie McNeal, *The Present Future: Six Tough Questions for the Church* (San Francisco: Jossey-Bass, 2003), 126.

14. See Chapter 6, *Grow into Your Original Design*.

15. There are several spiritual gifts assessments available online.

16. I use Gallup StrengthsFinder, the Myers-Briggs Type Indicator and Gifted2Serve Spiritual Gifts Inventory. For more information or to take these assessments contact me at henriet@TheStoryLives.com or visit TheStoryLives.com.

17. Matthew 22:16, NIV

18. Proverbs 2:7, NIV

19. Romans 5:3b-5, ESV

20. George Barna, *The Seven Faith Tribes: Who They Are, What They Believe, and Why They Matter* (Carol Stream, IL: Tyndale House Publishers, 2009), 129.

21. 1 Peter 5:2-3, NIV

22. 1 Peter 3:15, CEV

23. John 13:34-35, NLT

24. J. Robert Clinton and Richard W. Clinton, *The Mentor Handbook: Detailed Guidelines and Helps for Christian Mentors and Mentorees* (Altadena, CA: Barnabas Publishers, 1991), 17-1.

25. George Barna, *The Seven Faith Tribes: Who They Are, What They Believe, and Why They Matter* (Carol Stream, IL: Tyndale House Publishers, 2009), 193.

Chapter 10

Go Tell Your Story

God authorized and commanded me to commission you: Go out and train
everyone you meet, far and near, in this way of life, marking them by baptism
in the threefold name: Father, Son, and Holy Spirit. Then instruct them in the
practice of all I have commanded you. I'll be with you as you do this, day after
day after day, right up to the end of the age.

—Jesus[1]

The typical churched believer will die without leading a single person
to a lifesaving knowledge of and relationship with Jesus Christ.

—George Barna

The Disciples' Story Continued

Life with Jesus

Imagine life for Peter and John after Jesus left them. Over the course
of the three years of their lives with him, they had witnessed and been
an integral part of the greatest paradigm shift in history. They witnessed
Jesus moving people from law to grace. Along this journey, they were
transformed from simple fishermen with a heart for God to leaders in the
first Jesus movement known as *The Way*. The Church. From their first encounter with Jesus, they had experienced the highest highs and the lowest
lows. He had called them into a new life, and they had fully embraced
this new journey.

Like most invitations to a great adventure, they had started out with dreams and ideas of how their lives would play out. They chose to follow this leader and prophet who clearly came from God. Would they help him change the world? Would they be in his government? No one knows what they might have thought, but most likely they anticipated an exciting future ahead. Life with Jesus had been exciting, but this new life was different then anything they could have imagined.

It took years for them to comprehend that Jesus was the Messiah; the one they had been waiting for. They might have believed early on in the journey with Jesus that he was the Messiah, but they did not fully understand God's plans for the Messiah.

When they followed Jesus, they witnessed his power to transform lives, bring healing, raise people from the dead, set captives free, and bring hope to the hopeless. In the process, they too were changed.

Jesus addressed their character issues. John asked if he could sit at Jesus' right or left once he came into his Kingdom. John clearly was a leader, and he wanted to be in a position of power, next to his Lord. Jesus transformed him into the Apostle who talked and wrote about love.

Jesus also addressed character issues with Peter. He wanted to join Jesus in the supernatural, but he soon sank when the reality of stepping out of his boat and onto the rough sea set in and doubt erupted. Peter was daring, but he also was afraid of consequences. Jesus transformed Peter into a bold preacher and humble leader.

On the journey with Jesus, they experienced power, fulfillment, embarrassment, fear, doubt, and grief. They had walked away from the life they knew to follow him. Then he died. Had it all been a mistake?

John the Baptist had experienced the same doubt. "Are you the one or..." Even the one sent to prepare the way filled with doubt about Jesus. Why? Jesus didn't fit the traditional expectations. His approach to life made little logical sense to them. Jesus came as a servant, he suffered and died.

Consider how Jesus lived:
- He spent time with the wrong people by choosing to connect with those who were rejected, poor, ill, possessed, overlooked, and broken.

✎ His followers saw him break many of the religious rules.

✎ He refused positions of power and privilege.

✎ His followers witnessed his authority over the laws of nature.

Almost everything they had learned and understood before meeting Jesus changed. Jesus transformed everything they thought they knew. In many ways, up was down and down was up. The paradigm shift was immense and beyond their understanding.

All the disciples, but especially Peter and John, learned:

✎ humility, faith, and true strength;

✎ to stand up for their beliefs;

✎ to seek and understand the ways of their Lord; and

✎ to lead the Church.

Life with the Holy Spirit

After Jesus returned to his Father, the disciples waited as Jesus had instructed. They were faithful and continued to meet with the other disciples, both men and women, and they prayed in earnest. Those ten days of waiting for the promised Holy Spirit to come upon them must have seemed like a very long time. Waiting for two days after Jesus died, and before they saw him again, probably had felt like an eternity. Now he had left again, and this time it was for good—at least until his final return. They waited, but did they know what they were waiting for?

During this time of waiting, Peter took action. He led the group, and they chose another disciple to replace Judas. They prayed. They stayed together as a group. They waited.

Then Pentecost arrived, and God poured out his Holy Spirit. When he came upon them, they testified about Jesus in various languages, which were not their own. After the initial demonstration of the Holy Spirit's power in and through them, Peter preached his first public sermon, and God gave them a great harvest of 3,000 new believers. How exciting! How overwhelming. How do you care for 3,000 new people? What structures did they put in place? How did they live? How did life change?

We know they continued in their cultural practices, and they prayed at the temple during the Jewish prayer times. Their faith in Jesus transformed those practices, but they didn't entirely replace them. They didn't start a cultural revolution. They led a Jesus movement! The Apostles continued in Jesus' practices. As Jesus had gone, daily, to the temple to pray and to teach, they continued to go to the temple.

Following Pentecost and the pouring out of the Holy Spirit, the disciples lived and worked in the following ways:

- The temple is where they met with the church for prayer and teaching.

- Groups of followers also regularly met together in homes.

- They continued meeting as believers, teaching, sharing communion, and praying.

- They met within the cultural structures without trying to cause upheaval.

- They participated in the community, living a life of love, and demonstrating the truth of the Gospel.

- As Jesus had done, they lived among the people to demonstrate this new life.

People noticed their love for God, to each other, and to the community! God "added to their number daily those who were being saved."[2]

Their Missional Revolution

In the midst of the existing religious culture and practices, the disciples led a missional revolution. Through the power of the Holy Spirit, they brought a paradigm shift.

The Revolutionary mind-set is simple: Do whatever it takes to get closer to God and to help others to do the same. Obliterate any obstacle that prevents you from honoring God with every breath you take. Be such an outstanding example of the Christian faith that no one will question your heart or lifestyle…The Revolution is about recognizing that we are not called to go to church. We are called to be the Church.

—George Barna

Jesus initiated this shift by being God among the people. God with us, Immanuel. Rather than doing church, as it had been done, and by hanging out with the religious establishment, Jesus lived out a paradigm shift. He walked to and sat with the people where they were. He ministered to them in the ordinary of life. He touched them, healed them, spoke to them, listened to them, and taught them the truth of God. He shared the Good News.

Now the disciples continued this approach. They lived and met as believers in their communities, amongst their neighbors. They used the cultural and religious structures to bring the new way of Jesus. Rather than instigating a cultural revolution or religious revolt, they worked within the community to bring a new way of life. Jesus' followers shared everything in common. They loved each other. They were forgiven and free to follow Jesus. They learned about their Lord, and they lived out his teachings—in their daily lives and in their spiritual practices.

Remember the occasion when Peter and John walked to the temple, and they encountered a crippled beggar at the temple gate? We talked about him in Chapter 1. He had been at that gate, every day, for many years. This man had been there when Jesus went to the temple. This beggar probably had regularly seen them, and they had regularly seen him. Yet, he hadn't been one of the people Jesus chose to heal. Why? We're not told. Why was the encounter with Peter and John on this day different and why was it recorded in the Bible? Did the Holy Spirit prompt Peter and John? All we know is that this man, on that day, encountered Jesus through Peter's and John's lives and actions. He asked for money, as he did every day. They went to the temple, as they did every day. This day, Peter looked at him—really looked at him. I suspect the Holy Spirit prompted him to notice the man, as if for the first time. John also looked on him.

Peter stopped, and said to the man, "Look at us."

The beggar directed his attention solely to Peter and John, letting all the other potential donors slip past. He hoped this would make his day. He hoped they'd give him a big gift. I'm confident, he knew they were followers of Jesus. After all, this man hung out at this gate all the time. He must have seen them with Jesus. It would be hard to sit at the gate of the temple, day after day, and not know the pulse and happenings in town. He probably also knew that the people of *The Way* were generous. They shared so no one in their new community had need.

The beggar looked up at Peter and John, and he might have thought, *If I receive a good gift, I can get out of sitting in the hot sun, and maybe they'll carry me to lie down in the shade.*

Peter and John gave him the best gift of all, Jesus. They told this beggar even though they had no money, they could offer him something much better.

Then they said, "In the name of Jesus Christ of Nazareth, walk!"[3] Immediately, they helped him up, and the beggar was healed. He leaped up and began to walk. He walked with them. As soon as he had received the gift of life and healing, the beggar praised God, and he joined the church. They welcomed him into their fold.

The people recognized him as the crippled beggar who had pleaded for coins at the temple gate. His healing amazed them. Peter and John did not leave the healing and miracle open to people's individual interpretation or speculation. Peter used it to preach a fiery sermon that pointed to Jesus.

His sermon was not topical, feel-good, or seeker-sensitive. He told his Jewish audience they had killed the "author of life." He explained the beggar was healed not by their own power, but through the power of Jesus' name and the faith that comes through him.

Peter proclaimed, "Repent, then, and turn to God, so that your sins may be wiped out, that times of refreshing may come from the Lord, and that he may send the Christ, who has been appointed for you—even Jesus."[4]

This act of healing and the subsequent preaching followed the model Jesus had given his disciples. He had lived among the people, healing, and teaching. Now his disciples lived in the community, healing, and teaching. Following in their Master's footsteps, they continued to live both missionally and incarnationally—demonstrating Jesus' love and power through their lives and actions.

The people in the religious culture of that time placed this beggar at the temple gate day after day. They "brought" the beggar "to church" and he remained a beggar. He received help from people who were attending religious services, but he was never "reached" by them or included. Why would they? This man would have been considered judged by God.

Peter and John stopped on the way to "church" that day. They stopped and looked. They gave the beggar their attention, making him a valued person rather than an invisible outcast. They did what Jesus had done on so many occasions. Peter and John refused to put just a bandage on the man's problems. They saw his real need, and they offered him true life. They provided him with healing in Jesus' name. They shared their hope. They made Jesus real to this man, and he grabbed onto faith and life in Jesus with both hands.

Jesus told his disciples, and they taught their followers, to love God, and to love their neighbors. Through their lives and stories, they demonstrated the reality of Jesus to those who watched them. They loved each other. There were no needy persons among them. They lived in such a way that others wanted to join them.

Be a Community of Love

A cabin nestled in pine trees amidst freshly fallen snow was alive with the joy of people gathered together in the winter night. The room was warmed by logs crackling in the fireplace and oil lamps cast a cranberry glow. A group of friends sipped hot chocolate and apple cider. They ate from a long, pine table spread with a feast of lovingly prepared food. The friends laughed, enjoying each other's company. They were warm, content, and together.

Another group of people shivered on the path leading to the cabin, their feet frozen in the deep snow. The howling wind stung their cheeks. Ice stuck to their hair. A world of weariness had gripped their bodies. They pointed toward the cabin, seeing the warm glow through the window.

Laughter spilled from of the cabin. Aromas of cider and delicious food floated in the air and lifted the wanderer's noses, and their mouths watered for a taste. This group of shivering men, women, and children pressed their faces against the windows and witnessed the joy and heard the laughter. A pack of wolves howled in the distance.

The old man leading the way, knew some of his people wouldn't live to see the sunrise if they stayed in the cold. The joy, the food, and the warmth of those people gathered in the cabin created a deep longing. He craved to enter the cabin to secure food and safety for his entire group. His heart hungered for what they had. *If only,* he thought, *if only they' welcome us.*

The door swung open with a bang, and the love of those people gathered for fellowship, flowed from the cabin, and out into the winter night. They smiled and enveloped the shivering group with their love and woolen blankets. They invited them in to sit by the fire and eat their food.

In this scenario, how easy would it be to invite someone to come in and get warm and have something to eat and drink? Who would resist the offer to join the group and be included in the fun? The early church had this contagious effect on people.

Jesus' followers looked like the church and people wanted to join them. As a church today, wouldn't it be glorious to have this effect on people? We need to be and look like a fun and joyful group of people who are loving God, loving each other, and loving neighbors. If we resembled a warm cabin amid the cold snow of the needs and hardships of our communities, people would long for an invitation to join us. How can we get there? How can we spread that warmth so people long to come in out of the cold?

Tell Your Story through Your Actions

Let's allow people to see our love in action. Let them see us loving each other and loving them. As Jesus was sent by his Father, so he sent us—to live out his love and story. His story lives through us. As Christians, and especially as missional leaders, he calls us to live our stories missionally and incarnationally to reach people with his love.

Living missionally means living with the purpose of making Jesus known. Living missionally requires transparency and vulnerability. Jesus lived in the community. Let's follow his example, and live visibly and attractively among our neighbors and friends. It's important that each and every one of us live our stories.

We all have stories—whether we are aware of them or not. Living intentionally requires us to live our stories on purpose. What's that purpose? To be witnesses to the watching world to tell of God's love for everyone. Living intentionally requires us to keep our eyes open to where God is at work in us and around us. Being intentional requires us to accept God's invitation to join him where he is at work. How amazing is the truth that the God of the universe invites you and me to join him to make his love known to people who don't yet know him.

Why did God send Jesus? Why did Jesus give up his life with God in heaven? We know and believe, it was for the purpose of people coming to know God's love and through faith in Jesus have everlasting life. If we believe it, how can we not share it? Most of us know we "should" but often rely on pastors and professional ministers to tell people about Jesus. This wasn't Jesus' intention. He lived his story. He sent all of us, as his followers, to visibly live our stories—together. People can only read his story when we live it out together.

When we live our stories missionally together people will see and experience Jesus. Living missionally requires checking in with Jesus. It requires going into every day, every experience, and every encounter with our eyes open for opportunities to demonstrate Jesus' love. Maybe it's through a smile. Maybe it's through a simple act of kindness. Maybe it's by speaking a kind word. Maybe it's by sending a note or calling a friend who is alone. Maybe it's by helping a teen in trouble or bringing food to a neighbor. You get the picture.

Let us tell our stories together as we benefit those around us. One effective way we can live Jesus' story is through volunteering. It allows us to intentionally connect with people and serve them in Jesus' name.

To go tell as the Church, we need good leaders who guide us to live our stories and help us reset our priorities to align with Jesus' command to, "Go and make disciples." We need incentives to get us to go out instead of staying in.

Reggie McNeal tells us:
 The church needs to develop new scorecards, missional scorecards.[5]

⌘ We need to celebrate and count those activities that fit into the incarnational lifestyle, like conversations with neighbors, volunteering at local nonprofits, connecting in the community, and doing acts of kindness.

⌘ The scorecard needs to reflect the values of living our stories missionally and incarnationally.

Jesus commanded us to go and make disciples of all nations. People will only know if they hear or read our stories. They can only know our stories if we tell them. We need to know our stories and know ourselves in order to live our stories well. It's key we go tell, in order for people to experience Jesus. Together we are the Church. As the Church, we demonstrate Jesus' love, practically, when we invest our individual and collective stories in the community.

The direction is simple and clear. Jesus sends us out together to live missionally to reach people with his love.

Live Together as Jesus Intended

Imagine a community of people who live together as Jesus intended:

⌘ They know each other's names, as well as the needs.

⌘ They spend time together, share meals, participate in projects, and care for the children, as well as the sick.

⌘ They do this for their own Christian community, but they also do this for their neighbors.

⌘ This community actively volunteers at local nonprofits, intentionally connects with neighbors, and participates in the life of the community.

⌘ These believers can be counted on to help, as well as to pray.

⌘ Imagine the group being known for the laughter as well as their kindness.

⌘ When they hold a block party or community picnic, everyone wants to come because the food is great and plentiful, the care is genuine, and the laughter abundant.

Can you imagine this community? Could this be our community? Our churches? The Church? I imagine people would tell the story of this group of people. Then, through their stories, Jesus' story lives on.

> *The revolution starts with you, doing what you are capable of doing, regardless of what others are doing…You, personally, are responsible for revolutionizing the world. You cannot do it alone, but it cannot be done without you.*
>
> —George Barna

Living It Out

What about your story? You are the only you we will ever have. You're an important part of the overall community. You can only tell your story. Are you telling it? Are you living it? Don't just bury your story in a box on Sunday. Don't wait to tell it. Don't believe that you don't have a story to tell or that your story doesn't matter. Jesus sends you to tell your story so that others can become followers of Jesus. "God takes the initiative to invite you to be involved with him. When you obey him, he accomplishes his work through you in such a way that you and everyone else know God has been at work."[6] Tell your story so that people can see and hear what it means to be a disciple of Jesus. Be bold and say, with the Apostle Paul, "Follow my example, as I follow the example of Christ."[7]

Key Concepts

- As Jesus was sent, he sends us to live out his love and his story.
- Jesus' story lives through us.
- People can only read Jesus' story when the church lives it out together.
- To go tell, we need good leaders.
- All Christ-followers need to go do good intentionally and connect with others.
- Jesus lived his story. We need to live our stories to demonstrate the life and love of Jesus.

ᓚᑫ We need to know ourselves and our stories.

ᓚᑫ We need to go tell our stories together so that people may experience Jesus.

Questions for Living It Out

1. Do you know your story?

2. Are you telling your story? Are you telling your story with others?

3. How are you contributing to making sure Jesus' story lives?

4. What is your part in leading a missional revolution?

5. How has learning about Jesus' story challenged you to go tell your story?

Notes

1. Matthew 28:18-20, The Message

2. Acts 2:47, NIV

3. Acts 3:6, NIV

4. Acts 3: 19-20, NIV

5. Reggie McNeal, *Missional Renaissance: Changing the Scorecard for the Church* (San Francisco: Jossey-Bass, 2009), xvii.

6. Henry T. Blackaby and Claude V. King, *Experiencing God: How to Live the Full Adventure of Knowing and Doing the Will of God* (Nashville: Broadman & Holman Publishers, 1994), 173.

7. 1 Corinthians 11:1, NIV

Bibliography

Barrett, Lois Y., Darrell L. Guder, and Walter C. Hobbs. *Treasures in Clay Jars: Patterns in Missional Faithfulness*. Grand Rapids, MI: Wm. B. Eerdmans, 2004.

Barna, George. *Revolution*. Carol Stream, IL: Tyndale House Publishers, 2005.

—. *The Seven Faith Tribes: Who They Are, What They Believe, and Why They Matter*. Carol Stream, IL: Tyndale House Publishers, 2009.

Barton, R. Ruth. *Strengthening the Soul of Your Leadership: Seeking God in the Crucible of Ministry*. Downers Grove, IL: InterVarsity Press, 2008.

Blackaby, Henry T. and Claude V. King. *Experiencing God: How to Live the Full Adventure of Knowing and Doing the Will of God*. Nashville: Broadman & Holman Publishers, 1994.

Blackaby, Henry T. and Mel Blackaby. *What's So Spiritual About Your Gifts?* Colorado Springs, CO: Multnomah Publishers, 2004.

Blackaby, Henry T. and Richard Blackaby. *Spiritual Leadership: Moving People on to God's Agenda*. Nashville: Broadman & Holman Publishers, 2001.

Bosch, David J. *Believing in the Future: Toward a Missiology of Western Culture*. Valley Forge, PA: Trinity Press International, 1995.

Clinton, J. Robert and Richard W. Clinton. *The Mentor Handbook: Detailed Guidelines and Helps for Christian Mentors and Mentorees*. Altadena, CA: Barnabas Publishers, 1991.

Deere, Jack S. *Surprised by the Power of the Spirit: Discovering How God Speaks and Heals Today*. Grand Rapids, MI: Zondervan, 1993.

Gibbs, Eddie. *ChurchNext: Quantum Changes in How We Do Ministry*. Downers Grove, IL: InterVarsity Press, 2000.

Green, Joel B., Scot McKnight, and I. Howard Marshall. *Dictionary of Jesus and the Gospels*. Downers Grove, IL: InterVarsity Press, 1992.

Knippenberg, Hans, and Sjoerd de Vos. "Spatial Structural Effects on Dutch Church Attendance," *Wiley Online Library*. John Wiley & Sons, Inc., March 27, 2008 (first published online), http://onlinelibrary.wiley.com/doi/10.1111/j.1467-9663.1989.tb01733.x/abstract. First published in *Tijdschrift voor Economische en Sociale Geografie*, June 1989. Vol. 80. Issue 3. (30 August 2011).

Liddell, Henry G. and Robert Scott. *A Greek-English Lexicon*. New York: Oxford University Press, 1992.

McKnight, Scot. *The Jesus Creed: Loving God, Loving Others*. Brewster, MA: Paraclete Press, 2004.

McNeal, Reggie. *Missional Renaissance: Changing the Scorecard for the Church*. San Fancisco: Jossey-Bass, 2009.

—. *The Present Future: Six Tough Questions for the Church*. San Francisco: Jossey-Bass, 2003.

Newbigin, Lesslie. *The Open Secret: An Introduction to the Theology of Mission*. Grand Rapids, MI: Wm. B. Eerdmans Publishing Company, 1995.

Roxburgh, Alan J. and Fred Romanuk. *The Missional Leader: Equipping Your Church to Reach a Changing World*. San Francisco: Jossey-Bass, 2006.

Spurgeon, Charles H. "A Sermon and a Reminiscence," *Sword and the Trowel*, March 1873, www.spurgeon.org/s_and_t/srmn1873.htm (27 July 2012).

Stearns, Richard. 2009. *The Hole in Our Gospel*. Nashville: Thomas Nelson, 2009.

The Barna Group. "Donors Proceed with Caution, Tithing Declines." May 10, 2011, http://www.barna.org/donorscause-articles/486-donors-proceed-with-caution-tithing-declines?q=study+shows+trends+tithing+donating (29 September 2011).

Viola, Frank and George Barna. *Pagan Christianity?: Exploring the Roots of Our Church Practices*. Carol Stream, IL: Tyndale House Publishers, 2008.

About the Author

Henriët Schapelhouman seeks to live her story for Jesus. She longs to hear, "well done good and faithful servant" once she meets him face to face. Henriët has always sought to live purposefully. She loves creating order out of chaos, developing and directing teams and projects, and leading change.

Her work story is multifaceted. In 2007, while working on her masters degree in global leadership at Fuller Theological Seminary, and after she received a compelling vision about intentional Christian collaboration, Henriët founded Semper Vita. This Christian nonprofit organization exists to help people find their personal wiring so they can collaborate to bring the Good News to the community—living and leading missionally together. She is also an ordained Free Methodist pastor and serves as the executive director of Semper Vita.

Henriët also is the founder and president of Semper Vita Institute, a training company that uses StrengthsFinder, Myers-Briggs (MBTI) and spiritual gifts assessments to help business leaders discover and develop their personal wiring. She is a certified MBTI Practitioner and Certified Strengths Advisor.

She brings over 20 years of spiritual direction and team leadership experience in ministry-related positions to both organizations. Prior to these missional ventures, she worked at Timberlake Christian Fellowship in Redmond, WA, as pastor of adult ministries. Before Timberlake she had been pastor to women at Lincoln Glen Church in San Jose, CA. Henriët started her work story with a career in public relations for the high-tech and consumer sectors after graduating with a marketing degree.

Henriët has a master's degree in global leadership from Fuller Theological Seminary, Pasadena, California, and a bachelor's degree in business from the University of Santa Clara, Santa Clara, California. She's a popular speaker at conferences and retreats, and has conducted numerous training workshops and leadership classes. She's had several articles published and writes on her blog, www.henrietsblog.com. You can learn more about her published works, speaking schedule, and current projects at, www.henrietschapelhouman.com.

Henriët was born in the Netherlands and moved to the United States in 1979. A first generation American, she married, Fred, in 1981, and they have one son born in 1992. They reside in Redmond, Washington with their Boxer, Belle, and two cats, Torino and Mr. Boots. She enjoys taking long walks in the woods around her home, driving her two-seater, and gathering with friends and family.

More Praise for *The Story Lives*

We live in a world that wants to know whether Christianity is "for real." In this sense we are hungry for the stories of those who are living incarnationally. This book takes us into those stories and helps us to realize how we too can become a part of the story, impacting our world. You will want to dig into each chapter and find where you might be in the process of living out your story! Thank you Henriët for bringing us this resource.

Carla Sunberg
President
Wesleyan Holiness Women Clergy
Fort Wayne, Indiana

Henriët's book invites us to dive into leadership in fresh invigorating ways. Starting from a place of quiet rest with our God, we live into our call immersed in renewal and trust. As we listen for the Holy Spirit's direction from a place of quiet we are equipped to bring our entire team along for the journey. Missional ministry and living flow from a place of deep intimacy with God. I invite you to dwell with Henriët's words and experience transformation.

Rita Nussli
Spiritual Director
Soul Formation
Seattle, Washington

Taking the scary out of missional, this book encourages me to simply live my life and story for Jesus. I had always had the understanding that the word missional and going overseas went together. The Story Lives *helps you to understand that, "yes" going overseas is a part of being missional, but it's not all there is to it. We all can live out our life stories and be missional in our very own communities. This I can do!*

Cindy Patterson
Free Methodist Pastor and missional community leader
Redmond, Washington

Henriët Schapelhouman's passion to see Christ followers unleashed to serve the world and the church set free from harmful paradigms comes through loud and clear in "The Story Lives." A must read for anyone serious about their faith and living out what it means to be authentically Christian.

Matt Whitehead
Superintendent
Pacific Northwest Conference of the Free Methodist Church
Seattle, Washington

Discover How To
Fully Let Your Story Live
with Henriët Schapelhouman.

Bring The Story Lives *to your church, nonprofit, missional community, retreat or conference!*

Grow Event—Discover the Real You

Discover and develop your strengths and personality to unleash the real you, embrace your purpose and focus, and be the hands and feet of Jesus in your community. Through interactive learning activities, engaging presentations, group discussion, and personal reflection, you will learn about the Kingdom fit for your life story.

Full Day and Half Day Workshops or One Topic Talks

With several offerings to choose from, Henriët will share her expertise in missional living, personality discovery, and leadership, to provide a combination of transformational presentations and interactive learning. Sample topics include:

+ Missional Volunteering: Let's Take the Church Out of the Box
+ Five Easy Steps to Live Missionally
+ Discover Missional Community: Models, Guidelines and Simple Practices
+ Moving Beyond the Box: Follow Jesus' Example to Love Your Neighbor
+ Taking Your Story Out of the Church and Into the Community

Speaking, Teaching and Guest Preaching

Inspire your congregation or group to fully engage in Jesus' Kingdom and easily answer the Great Commission. Through biblically-based, story-filled, practical messages, Henriët will encourage and challenge your church or group to fully live into their identity as authentic Christ-followers.

Visit TheStoryLives.com *for full descriptions of available offerings and how to attend or host an opportunity near you.*

Share your story — *Are you living your story for Jesus?*
Tell your story on TheStoryLives.com and share the journey. Submit your story about how you are actively living out Jesus' love to your family, friends, neighbors and beyond. Be part of the Missional Revolution and inspire others.
Join our online community today.